Haunted Iowa

KATHLEEN VYN

HAUNTED IOWA

Copyright © 2018 by Kathleen Vyn

All rights reserved.

No part of this book may be reproduced or transmitted in any form or by any means, graphic, electronic, or mechanical, including photocopying, recording, taping, or by any information storage or retrieval system, without the permission in writing from the publisher.

Published by Heathcliff Press

Print ISBN: 9781625361288
Ebook ISBN: 9781625361271

*To my great-grandmother, Libbie,
and everyone who knows that
there's more to the world
than what we see.*

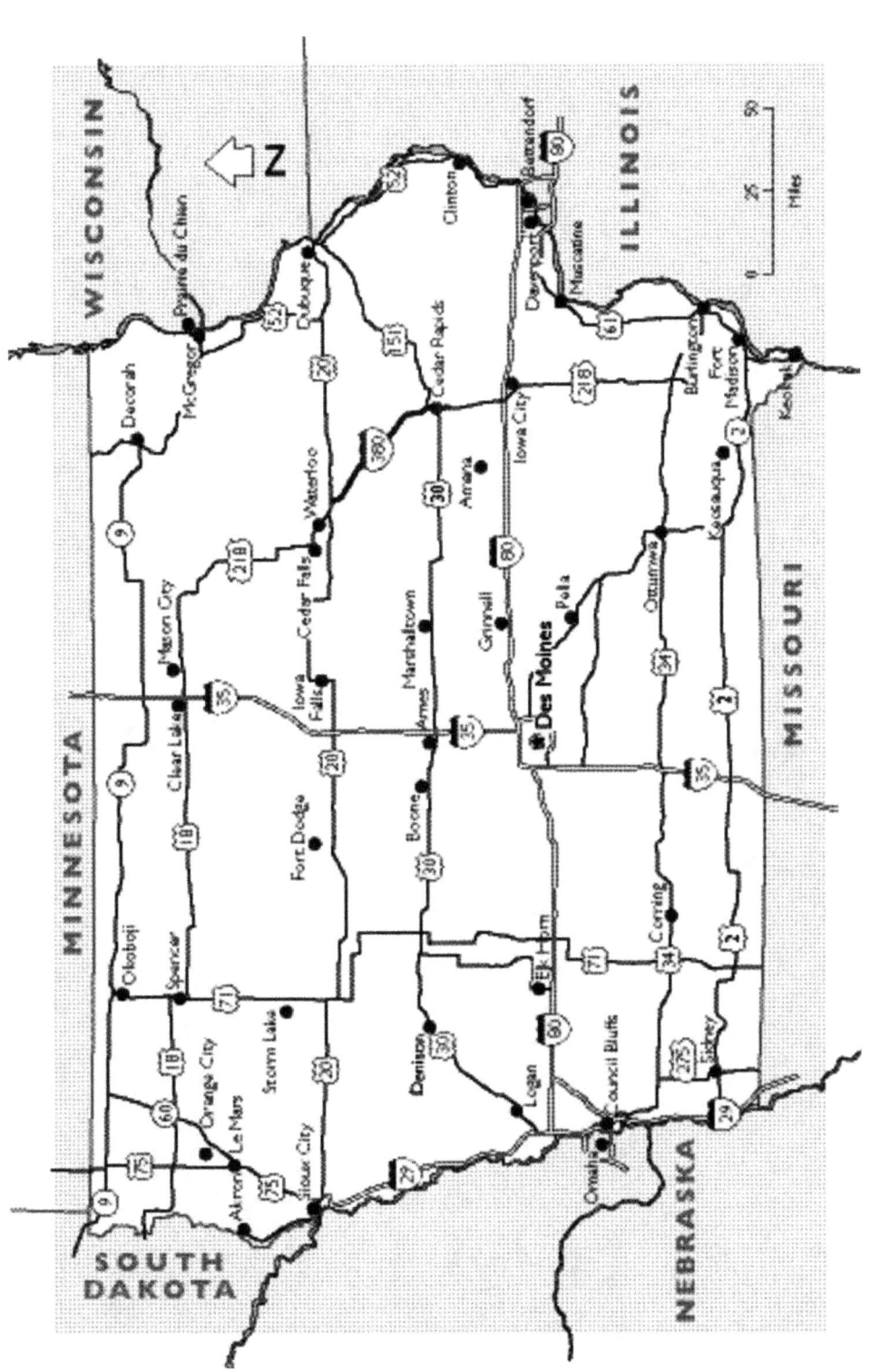

Acknowledgments

I wish to thank these Iowans who shared their stories with me. Without their generosity, this book could not have been written.

JOE LETO, founder of DIEPART, who shared his vast knowledge of the paranormal with me.

THE DIEPART TEAM MEMBERS, who were always gracious and helpful: Shannon Kingrey, Kellie Wilmot, Dan Gifford, Terri Smith, Dan Berger, Jennifer Rice, and Lynne Goodwin.

BRAD STEIGER, who took time out for an interview when he had deadlines and radio interviews scheduled.

RICK AND CINDY NELSON, owners of the Carter House; Judy Salier who gave me the fascinating details of the haunting of the Monroe Mansion, the Victorian house where she and her family lived.

THANKS ALSO TO: Bruce Carlson, publisher, Quixote Press; Annette Hacker, University Relations, Iowa State University; David Ross, Des Moines, former owner of Natural History Tours Iowa; Randa LeJeune, owner of Historic Gaslight Ghost Tours; Susan Jellinger, librarian for the State Historical Society of Iowa; John Hayes, historian; Gordon Kellenberger and Lanny Haldy, Amana Colonies; Cynthia Dyer, librarian archivist, Simpson College; Jerry Hopkins, Cedar Rapids Public Library; Professor Phil Hey, Briar Cliff College; Katie Giorgio, Membership and Communications, Cedar Rapids Museum of Art; Tina Carlson, co-director of The Shadowlands; and Tacie Campbell with the Dubuque County Historical Society.

Introduction

Do you believe in ghosts? Thousands of Iowans do; they've lived with the strange noises, the mysteriously moving objects, the eerie premonitions, and the stranger in odd clothes who appears for a moment and then vanishes. Iowa may be long on cornfields and short on windswept heaths or spooky forests, but Iowans hold their own with anyone in the ectoplasm category. In fact, some Iowans believe in ghosts so strongly that they've dedicated themselves to the task of documenting the existence of spirits from beyond walking among us.

Many of the ghost stories in this book have never been published before. Many are from the case files of the Iowa Paranormal Advanced Research Team (IPART), which is affiliated with The Atlantic Paranormal Society, the group that created the TV series *Ghost Hunters*. This book includes the stories of DIEPART (Des Moines, Iowa, Extreme Paranormal Advanced Research Team) groups from Sioux City to Iowa City that have had paranormal encounters during the course of their investigations. The IPART team protects the privacy of its clients. In most of the stories I've included, the names of people who have had paranormal experiences have been changed.

Joe Leto, the founder of DIEPART (Des Moines, Iowa, team), explained how a professional paranormal research team works. A team can consist of as many as twelve trained investigators using a variety of high-tech equipment to document the traces of visitors from the other side. When the team begins an investigation on a site, the members set up camp and spend the night collecting data, using tools both scientific and simple. First they set up infrared cameras throughout the house. Then they tape Mylar strips on strategic places to capture movement. (These are controlled experiments that Joe calls "building a better mousetrap." The infrared cameras catch the moving apparitions as they set off the film strips.) After they've gathered the data, the team spends six or seven hours analyzing it. They call the process "chronicling and reporting."

According to Joe, the problem with hunting for ghosts is that you can't turn paranormal activity on and off. Sometimes it happens, but more often than not it doesn't. The cases I've included in *Haunted Iowa* are some of the DIEPART team's strongest cases. Many of the people who experienced the hauntings later became members of the team. These stories are still unfolding. They don't have a conclusion.

DIEPART never charges its clients for its investigations. In fact, they see the biggest part of their mission as providing help to people who must deal with unexplained experiences. Often when a ghost invades a house, the household is turned upside down. Family members are awakened in the night by weird noises. Needed objects are mysteriously missing. Whole rooms of the house can become uninhabitable. DIEPART is there to help them with this kind of intolerable situation. Once or twice a week, team members spend nights at the house gathering data and helping clients rid themselves of ghostly invaders. Think of it as a kind of metaphysical exterminator service.

Along with the best of the DIEPART cases, this book includes Iowa folktales and descriptions of haunted sites. Since Iowa has been a rural state with a long history, it's natural that the state would be rich with ghost stories. Iowa is filled with old cemeteries, mansions, and historic buildings. Many of the folk stories I've included are in the tradition of ghost stories that have been handed down from generation to generation. I interviewed dozens of people around the state to gather these stories and included the best ones here.

It's not just the story; it's the experience. Whether or not you believe in the hereafter, you'll understand how people process their paranormal experiences. You'll learn about interactive ghosts—ghosts that talk to the people in the houses they haunt and follow them from place to place; spiritual pranksters that move objects around the house; ghosts that dislike dogs so much that they lift the family dog out of the window and onto the porch. There are shadow men, ghosts that appear out of the corner of the eye, then disappear; other ghosts become so material that you can actually touch them.

In the last section of the book, I have included interviews with Iowans who are on the cutting edge of the paranormal. Many of them have been involved with such unexplained phenomena all of their lives, having grown up in haunted houses and led tours of haunted sites in their towns. Native Iowan Brad Steiger is the author of more than 165 books on the paranormal, which have sold more than 17 million copies. He and his wife, Sherry Hansen Steiger, have written 22 books as a team. After living all over the country, they have chosen to return to the Hawkeye State to continue their investigations into the realm of the unexplained.

Steiger talks about how growing up in Fort Dodge, Iowa, led him to his career in the paranormal. He was a writer about the paranormal before it was fashionable; Steiger's first story was published in 1956. "When I began investigating hauntings in the late 1950s, research had to be done with the secrecy of the Manhattan Project," he said. Since then he has had over two thousand magazine articles published on such subjects as ghosts, UFOs, unknown archaeology, and spirituality. He was one of the founding contributors to the influential journal of the paranormal, *Fate*. His book *Atlantis Rising* was given five stars by Scott Corales of *Inexplicata—the Journal of His-panic Ufology*.

Steiger also talks about his recent collaborations with Sherry, who is a medicine woman and an ordained Protestant minister. His investigations with his wife have led him into a deep understanding of the transition between life and death, which the two have shared in their inspirational series for cable television *Could It Be a Miracle?*

Also included is an interview with Des Moines, Iowa, resident Randa LeJeune, who lives in a house haunted by three ghosts. She runs Historic Gaslight Ghost Tours, leading guests on walking expeditions to as many as ten spooky sites in Des Moines.

I spoke to Wever, Iowa, resident Bruce Carlson, who is the publisher of Quixote Press. He has published and written books about haunted sites in his collections entitled *Ghosts of Scott County, Iowa* and *Ghosts of Des Moines County, Iowa*. He's been acquainted with the paranormal side of Iowa all of his life.

I've included familiar Iowa ghost stories such as Sonny, Kate Shelley, the Millville Ghost, the Black Angel, the Grand Opera, Villisca, and Alfie the Pig. But there are also obscure haunted locations and cemeteries that I'll bet you've never heard of before.

Perhaps you've had your own encounter with someone or something from the other side. If so, I hope you'll be able to relate to the stories you read here. But my chief hope is that readers who have never had a paranormal encounter of their own will be able to get a sense of what it's like to experience something so uncanny, something undeniably real yet utterly inexplicable. Our experience of daily life is often so limited by our mundane expectations that we forget that the universe is full of mystery and we don't really understand more than a tiny fraction of it. These unexplained incidents are a wake-up call to us that the marvelous is out there, waiting to be explored.

Is your spine tingling? That could be the promise of a strange and fantastic adventure right around the corner.

The DIEPART Team

Haunting Sparks New Career

Joe Leto, the founder of DIEPART, is a technology nerd. An electronic ham radio operator since he was a kid, he had the highest-level FCC license at the age of 12. He received a degree in radio frequency engineering from the University of Iowa. After a six-year stint in the Navy, he was a field manager for a Des Moines telephone company. His next job was chief engineer for a TV station and a media producer for Captain Jack Films.

Dealing every day with the certainties of electronic engineering gave Joe a matter-of-fact frame of mind. "I never believed in ghosts or anything supernatural," says Joe. "I never even thought about it. I don't watch scary movies. I'm not into that stuff."

But when Joe and his wife and daughters moved into a small rental house in Winterset, Iowa, in the spring of 2003, a series of events occurred that would change his worldview and set him on an entirely new career path.

Shortly after they settled into the house, his daughters came to him crying and said they were hearing voices.

"They told me the voices were telling them to do terrible things: 'push your sister down the stairway,' 'get into the utensils and stab someone.' The voices came any time of the day, even at three or five a.m. My wife and I didn't know what was wrong."

At first, Joe discounted his daughters' disturbing reports, but an experience of his own soon convinced him they were telling the truth. One day when he was on his way to work, he realized he had forgotten to bring his soda along for lunch. "I ran back to the house and unlocked the door," says Joe. "When I got inside and walked in the kitchen, I saw the refrigerator door open, cupboard doors wide open, and utensils on the table. The stove door was open. It was then I started to believe what my kids were telling me."

His daughter was so scared she came to him with her little hands cupping her ears. She didn't want to hear the voices anymore.

Trying to find out what was going on, Joe learned that the house they were renting was originally an Episcopal church built in 1890 that had been moved to the site and remodeled to become a rental property. "This was your funeral church," says Joe, "where you get married, baptized." The apex of the house, which used to be the steeple, was jagged, and the cornice was torn.

Joe, who is a Catholic, asked his pastor if he could help him get rid of the spirits, but the undoubtedly skeptical priest said there was nothing he could do. Joe's brother-in-law suggested they open up all the doors and windows in the house, then demand whatever was residing there to leave. As Joe issued his commandment, he felt an inexplicable rush of wind.

"We didn't hear the spirit for the next two years," says Joe.

Joe and his family moved away several years later, and the house was eventually torn down. But Joe's experience with the poltergeist led him to wonder if the electronic devices he was familiar with could be used to document the presence of unseen spirits. He had learned enough about radio technology to apply it to his paranormal research. After the house was torn down, he came back to Winterset.

"I had the overwhelming urge to see if there was anything remaining after so many years," says Joe.

He knew he could get physical evidence of the ghosts by taping their voices. With an amplified parabolic microphone, he walked around recording. "I heard a raspy voice calling, 'Joe,'" he said. "Then it kept telling me to push the button down harder. When you push it too hard, your finger starts aching. Soon mine did."

When Joe took his recording back home, he discovered that there were voices on the tape. He heard the same raspy voice calling his name. His parabolic microphone had worked. It had picked up sounds that other equipment couldn't. Joe knew he could pioneer paranormal research using this technology. In 2005, Joe founded the DIEPART group. He used his knowledge of radio equipment to improve the quality of the recordings they would gather at haunted sites.

Instead of being scared of the paranormal, Joe is excited about it. The DIEPART group isn't there to bust ghosts, he says. Instead, they come to validate what the client says. They always conduct their investigations professionally and with a scientific perspective.

In just two of their investigations, the DIEPART team has collected over 500 voices from the dead. They now use Joe's own invention, a parabolic microphone that is so sensitive it records sounds that other equipment can't pick up—even the proverbial pin drop.

According to Joe, DIEPART is pushing everything to the extreme, to build a better mousetrap. "It's our goal to keep trying new things to prove or disprove that the supernatural exists."

• • •

Since the first edition of *Haunted Iowa* was published in September of 2008, Joe Leto of DIEPART quit the ghost hunting business. He sold the company to Dan Berger and his wife.

"It wears on your family," says Joe, a father of two. "You're gone all weekend."

Now that Joe is working as a key operator at a local casino, he can spend more time with his family. He still gets calls from people who are having problems with ghosts, however. Most of them are afraid of ghosts.

He suggests they use a camera. "A camera gives a sense of protection and normalcy," he says. "In 99 percent of the cases, nothing happens while the camera is locked and loaded."

According to Joe, ghosts don't appear automatically. "I've been some of these places that are supposed to be quite scary. I'm a skeptic. I don't really find a lot to exaggerate over. You can't turn on ghostly activity like a faucet. A boy who hears voices needs to watch less scary movies at night."

Since this book was first published, Joe lost his mother and DIEPART member Lynne Goodwin, who was interviewed in "Chased by a Ghost." He's been trying to communicate with both of them.

High-Tech Ghost Hunting

"It should be observed that no living person knows, with absolute certainty, what becomes of human or animal consciousness after the inevitable cessation of biological life." So says the website of the Iowa Paranormal Advanced Research Team (IPART). But they don't let this inescapable fact prevent them from trying to find out. Real-life ghost hunters, complete with uniforms and gizmos, IPART teams use high tech to try to get to the world beyond, often borrowing techniques and equipment from mainstream realms of scientific investigation.

Joe Leto brought his background in radio technology to bear in developing new equipment for recording paranormal phenomena. "We decided we didn't want to do what other groups did. We're trying to advance the science of equipment technology," says Joe. "I want to think we're progressing on a scale that's never been seen before."

As a graduate of the University of Iowa in radio frequency engineering, Joe is an experienced astronomer and ham radio operator with a solid grounding in electronics. "I've done astronomy for over twenty years," says Joe. "What we do is like radio astronomy."

The IPART teams set up parabolic microphones to amplify audible frequencies, searching for the moans, cries, whispers, and other tell-tale sounds that often accompany ghostly manifestations. They make a digital recording of the session and then analyze it with special software, looking for sounds in the range between 54 kilohertz and 1.7 hertz, covering the entire audible spectrum, as well as inaudible vibrations above and below. "We pick up the faint and fuzzies," Joe says. A single recording session can generate six to eight hours of audio to analyze. The team is searching for "electronic voice phenomena," or EVPs, voices and other sounds that are inaudible in real time but mysteriously appear on the recording.

Unlike some ghost-hunting teams, IPART doesn't use filters and other tricks to "clean up" the sound on their super-sensitive recordings. A file that's been altered, says Joe, sounds tinny and robotized. "It's like an investigator that's changed the crime scene, stabbed the body more times. It changes the evidence. We don't allow our audio files to be changed or monkeyed with. We keep it pristine and real, not manufacturing evidence."

Using Joe's method, IPART gets 10 to 50 EVPs at each location. "Other organizations never get any," Joe says.

Another physical manifestation the IPART teams seek out is changes in electromagnetic fields, which paranormal investigators have long associated with supernatural phenomena. An apparition's movement can be tracked by following this change in radiation patterns. To measure such fluctuations, the team uses electromagnetic field (EMF) meters.

Joe's theory is that strong electromagnetic fields related to emotions amplify the paranormal. "A strong emotion that lasts for a period of time will imprint itself with an EMF," he says. "With the Villisca house murders, which happened in 1912, before there were electrical power plants, we found we couldn't get EMF readings. It's like taking the batteries out of a recorder. If there are power plants nearby, they can interfere with EMFs. So in order to get good EMFs, go to a cemetery far away from power plants, you can measure them coming in short bursts."

In many of their cases, the owners tell the DIEPART team that they've seen a ghost passing through the halls of their home. Joe devised a way of detecting the movement by placing an EMF meter on every other step on a stairway every 12 to 30 meters. "We created an EMF catwalk in one house where a woman saw a ghost coming up a stairway, walking through the hallway, and entering the bathroom," Joe says. "Our meters confirmed what she said. Each meter was set off, lighting up, then shutting off—boom boom. The sound notified us that something was happening. We got it all on film."

The problem with measuring electromagnetic fields is that stray voltage can come from anywhere—magnets in refrigerators, microwaves, and other household items, for example—and completely throw off meter readings. During an investigation of a former crack house outside of Des Moines, the team was excited to see EMF meters going off the charts—until they discovered that the anomaly was caused by a malfunction at a nearby power station. When the electric company fixed the problem, the levels went down.

"We've found that EMFs actually amplify the EVPs," says Joe. "If a house isn't properly grounded, the levels of EMFs can skyrocket."

One of the most common physical manifestations of a haunting is a change in temperature, the sudden chill that makes your hair stand on end. The DIEPART team uses thermal couplers that measure temperature changes in a room. They've been able to document drops of as much as 30 degrees, indicating that something is sucking energy out of the room. Some sites have gotten so cold that investigators have been able to see their breath.

The clearest sign that a house is haunted is when physical objects appear, move, change, and disappear, apparently on their own; ghost hunters refer to such phenomena as elementals. Poltergeists are noisy ghosts, created by telekinesis from a young person who lives in the house. Sometimes objects will move on their own, flying in the air. Doors slam. Pictures levitate.

One particularly weird example of an elemental involved a man who contacted DIEPART in 2007 searching for an explanation for something that happened to him in the middle of one strange night. His radio shorted out at about four a.m. Later that morning, a friend called to tell him that his brother had drowned while scuba diving in Florida. He looked in his radio and found salt water inside it. Aside from the radio, the night table had been empty.

Elementals are rare. To date, the DIEPART team has only had one investigation—an elemental at a site called the Water House, at which gallons of water came out of the air despite the absence of any pipes nearby. "An elemental is not a ghost or a poltergeist," says Joe. "It's fire, wind, water, soil. Basically, you wake up and find a pile of soil on the floor beside your bed. Wind blows through your bedroom. Little fires start all over the house."

Perhaps the most common ghostly phenomena are visual manifestations, which raises the question of how ghost hunters see in the dark when they investigate cases. They use the same technology as military and law enforcement agencies that need to pierce the darkness: infrared equipment. "It takes at least two hours for your night vision to begin working, fifteen hours to get the rest of your vision. So we use infrared lights, which enable us to see in the dark without compromising night vision," says Joe.

The team's infrared cameras record everything, even in a completely dark room, and display it as either a gray or green image. Each floor is set up with 12 cameras and a monitor, with computers recording everything digitally.

Joe often uses a photographic technique that he invented himself called Lighted Energy Tactical Observation (L.E.T.O). "We take Mylar strips and weight them with lead at the bottom. We position them on the ceiling with duct tape and pins. If a ghost passes through in the middle of the night, the Mylar strips reflect the infrared light and the cameras photograph the movement. The place lights up like the Fourth of July," says Joe. "I tell the other investigators, 'Don't tell me that those strips are just moving'—that could result from positive ventilation. I want to see those things swing like a hippy through beads."

The DIEPART team also uses other controlled experiments throughout the house to see whether objects move on their own. For example, Joe advised a woman from Rutland, Iowa, who suspected her house was haunted to put a circle of coins in a closed room. When she later returned to the room, she found that her array had been moved. She tried the experiment again, and the same thing happened. Finally, one day she watched her purse fly across the room. Her husband, sitting on the opposite side of the room reading his paper, hadn't even looked up at her. When the ghost slapped her on her thigh, the woman no longer had doubts that she had company.

She knew something unexplainable had happened to her. That's what happens to many people who try to find rational explanations for paranormal phenomena. Sometimes there just isn't any way to explain their experiences. It's only then that they understand that they've probably seen a ghost. No one really know for sure, however, what a real haunting is. It's usually just a set of experiences that can't be explained any other way.

Growing Up with Ghosts

Twenty-seven-year-old Shannon Kingrey grew up in a haunted house on the east side of Des Moines, Iowa. Her fascination with the supernatural would one day lead her to join DIEPART as a certified ghost investigator. As a young girl in 1989, Shannon saw an apparition that she couldn't explain: a mysterious companion.

"It was startling," says Shannon. "The first time I saw a ghost was when I closed the mirrored door of our bathroom. I saw her in the mirror behind me. She was sitting in the room watching me. I was upstairs on the second floor hallway, so it couldn't have been a reflection from a television or anything."

Shannon's mother had already encountered the little brunette girl standing across the dining room table from her. She realized it wasn't one of her daughters.

In fact, it soon became apparent that there were not one but two unexplainable inhabitants sharing their house with them. "They always appeared around the attic," says Shannon. "A lot of times when we were leaving, we'd see the two girls in the attic window looking down at us. It was very eerie, but it became very normal. They never interacted with us."

Shannon's little sister played with an invisible imaginary friend when she was four or five years old. "She had one of those little friends playing there with her. But there was nobody there," says Shannon.

"When I was thirteen, I used to collect those little troll dolls," says Shannon. "I had one ten inches tall from the '60s or '70s; if you pressed its stomach it would talk. I was sleeping one night and was awakened by the troll doll. My mother, who was downstairs, thought I was playing with it. I was still half asleep, and my mom came up the stairs, put on the light, and asked what I was doing. The sound and the light woke me up. That's when I noticed that the doll had fallen off of the shelves and its stomach was pressed in. I saw a depression in the toy. My mother freaked out about it. She told me to knock it off 'cause I had school the next day."

After the troll incident, the family was free for three years. Then one time when the whole family was together for the holidays, something strange occurred. "We had a glass front door in the living room that led to the outdoors. We had forty people together. We all saw the front porch light flip on. There's nobody out there turning it on. Instead of someone walking through the door, the glass fogged over. It was cold outside, like breath on the glass. It stayed that way for a second; then the lights shut off. We got up and inspected it to see what was going on. Nobody was out there. Forty people witnessed it at the same time."

Despite her own unexplained encounter, Shannon prides herself on being a skeptical investigator. She estimates that more than half of the testimony she hears from supposed haunting victims is simply bogus.

"We've found people faking evidence," says Shannon. "Then we can't believe anything they say. We leave. We feel sorry for these people; in some cases, the majority of the activity they report is fake." Still, the fact that the DIEPART team doesn't document any evidence of a haunting isn't proof that something strange hasn't been occurring at the site.

• • •

Orbs are phenomena that paranormal researchers often discover in haunted sites. These lights move through a room, pass through solid objects, then reappear. One case that Shannon investigated with other DIEPART investigators made her see that orbs are real. At about one a.m., sitting in a dark room upstairs in a house, she saw an orb of light about the size of a softball going up and down the stairs. Joe later told Shannon that he saw the orb, too. He followed it to the top of the stairs. Just as he did that, Shannon, while carrying an EMF recorder, followed the orb until it finally crossed her face, right into her nose. She dropped the equipment she had in her arms. At that moment, the orb jumped ahead of her, turning right, then left, into the bathroom before it disappeared into a hallway wall. There were no windows in the hallway.

Soon, investigators Irish and Terri, along with the rest of the DIEPART team, saw the orb. "I can't explain orbs," says Joe. "If you capture an orb on film and you don't see it with your eyes, then it's just dust. It's too easy to mistake. That is our whole stance. Orbs are so controversial. I've been able to debunk 99 percent of orb photos."

Then, on the Polk County investigation, several years ago, Shannon took a photo of an orb. "On the small LED screen of a digital camera, it looked real. But it wasn't." The orb was just a piece of dust flying through the air.

"We have thousands of photos from hundreds of cases," says Joe. "We have one or two that we'd consider real paranormal. We're very critical of our evidence. One picture does not make a paranormal case. It won't convince anyone. Some of the audio files we get are EVPs. They only last one or two seconds."

Orbs aren't the only phenomena paranormal investigators find. Often investigators capture sounds on their digital recorders. In a Des Moines house, the DIEPART team captured over 60 voices in one second. The house also had a strong electromagnetic field (EMF) radiating through it. Joe went outside to check for EMFs there, and he found that the electric meters were going to ten kilowatts, the highest they could go. A normal house should have a reading of zero. Joe found a transformer that wasn't grounded. This created an electromagnetic field, magnetic energy in a form you can pick up with a meter.

When Joe got back, he played the recordings. On it, a voice said, "What a greedy thing, man and oh. Hey kids, what's going on, get some crack." Joe was shocked. He didn't know that this house was a crack house. Neither did the other members of the team.

"I was surprised, too," says Shannon. "It's not that I'm not skeptical. In most cases, the strange activity can be explained."

Shannon suggests that people should keep a journal of the paranormal experiences they're having. "And if you're still having problems, call DIEPART."

Echoes of Ghosts

Dan Gifford's mother always explained strange events at their Humboldt County farm by saying "the ghosts did it." It's no wonder Gifford became an IPART member, then later regional manager.

"The faucet came on by itself when nobody was in the kitchen," says Gifford. "When we turned it off, we turned the handle six revolutions so it wouldn't turn on. But it did, anyhow. Other strange things happened there. It was as if someone was bumping into my mothers' hanging plants. She just said, 'The ghosts did it.'"

When Gifford got older, he began watching *Ghost Hunters*, the cable television show that began in the late '90s. He decided he wanted to be a paranormal investigator. He contacted Joe Leto at DIEPART.

"After meeting with Joe, I found that our philosophies were a lot alike," says Gifford. "We both try to find natural explanations for things. First we try to be a casual observer. We don't interact with the client. We put up our audio and video equipment and just observe. We don't take too much stock in orbs. Many things can cause them, like bugs or dust. But we did see them on our investigation in Fairbury, Nebraska. We all saw them."

After Fairbury, one of Gifford's most fascinating Iowa cases was an old farmhouse in Keokuk. The 26-room house, built in the 1850s, stands on a vast expanse of farmland. The wind blows around it constantly. The few trees bend in the unrelenting wind. Many people who lived there used to blame the wind for the strange phenomena they observed. But by the time Gifford and the DIEPART team went there in 2007, the people who were living in the house wanted confirmation of what they'd observed. Once they started renovating the kitchen and the living room, they saw an apparition of a black cat. Sometimes they'd feel the cat rubbing against their legs. By the time they bent down to touch it, it was gone. They also saw an apparition of a man in overalls staring at them, as though he was waiting for their approval. Soon afterward, the doors would slam on their own. Or they'd hear footsteps.

"When the Mitchells [the owners] spoke to their neighbors, they found out that there had been two murders in the house," says Gifford. "Another owner died in the garden of an apparent heart attack."

One day when the Mitchells' daughter was in her bedroom, their calico cat came running into it at full speed, as though he had seen something. She used a couple of pillows to prop the door open. Still, the door slammed shut.

When the DIEPART team came to the house, they heard the front door open. No one was out on the porch.

"I had the feeling that someone was watching me," says Gifford.

None of the members were laughing; they were riveted by the events. They were even more alert when one of the candlesticks Mr. Mitchell had put in the window suddenly flew across the room. The rest of the candlesticks disappeared. It was as though the ghost was afraid the unlit candles could cause a fire.

After the team set up their equipment, the Mitchells retreated to their own room. They locked up their two cats so they wouldn't disturb the DIEPART investigation.

"We pointed our camera in the daughter's bedroom, hoping to record the pillows moving," says Gifford. "Nothing happened. We're continuing our investigation."

Since true hauntings are rare occurrences, the paranormal investigators have to continue their research. Often one visit to a haunted site isn't enough. The Keokuk investigation is still open. The team barely had a chance to investigate the 26 rooms where apparitions have been observed.

When Gifford returns home to Fairfield, where he lives with his wife, he's returning to another haunted house. He seldom has any peace there.

"Whenever my wife and I would have a heated discussion, the overhead fan stopped moving," says Gifford. "It was as though it was telling us to stop arguing. When my wife spoke to our neighbor, she told her that our house was haunted."

The woman who lived there before them was a Wiccan, a member of a group that engages in various pagan religious practices. Sometimes the woman would plant the garden in the middle of the night. "Wiccans are more gentle witches, not ones that conjure. They're very connected to the seasons and nature," says Gifford.

Today, the plants in the garden seem to grow without any help. It's as if the Wiccan woman is overseeing their growth, guiding them to lush health.

Scared by a Ghost

MARSHALLTOWN, IOWA

Marshalltown is full of history. Located in central Iowa, it has many historic buildings, including an old blacksmith shop and the Susie Sower Heritage Homestead. But these sites didn't have what one simple duplex had.

To begin with, the Marshalltown duplex apartment had a sordid history. A murder had occurred there just 10 years before the Smith family moved in. The first two months of the Smiths' residence in their new home were uneventful. Then the parents began receiving strange reports from their children. Jason, a little boy, told his mother he had seen a monster. When she asked him what it looked like, he told her that it had dark hair and eyes. Later, his sister Sara saw a plate fly off the microwave. She jumped out of the way in time so it didn't hit her and ran crying to her mother.

The children weren't the only ones experiencing weird events. Mrs. Smith found the kitchen door ajar after she had just closed it. Then she heard footsteps on the stairs. No one was there. She turned off a light in the bedroom, and it turned back on by itself. Then in the middle of the night, her daughter heard someone say, "Hey." She jumped out of bed and ran into the parents' bedroom and stayed with them for the rest of the night. In spring of 2007, Mrs. Smith called the DIEPART team.

Joe said that the murder that had occurred in the Smith home a decade earlier was no simple homicide. "A woman killed a man there," Joe said. "He put up a good fight, but he died just the same. The woman was charged with murder. The police didn't have enough evidence to convict her. She escaped and hasn't been seen to this day."

The little boy described to Joe the monster he had seen: dark shadows shaped like a man. He had even spoken to the man; the shadowy form asked the boy why he stayed in the house, then screamed at him to leave. Jason began crying. He was so scared he couldn't go back into the room.

Joe showed him a photo. Jason said it was the man who had threatened him. In fact, it was a photo of the man who was murdered there. He had dark hair and dark eyes and an unsmiling, stern face.

The Smiths weren't the only ones hearing unexplained sounds. While investigating, DIEPART team-member Shannon heard a knocking sound in the basement and a disembodied voice whispering in the bedroom.

While the Smiths were pleased that the DIEPART team confirmed their experiences, they couldn't endure any more sleepless nights. Finally, the Smith family moved out. Though the apartment is vacant today, the ghost still lives there, waiting for a new unsuspecting family to move in.

Chased by a Ghost

When Lynne Goodwin and her family moved from Fairbury, Nebraska, to Iowa two years ago, they never imagined that a ghost would follow them to their new home in Des Moines.

They had barely survived an assault by ghosts at their rental home in Fairbury, a house that had been built in the early nineteenth-century. Lynne, who was originally from Dallas, Texas, had never had a paranormal experience prior to moving to Nebraska with her husband, Tom, who worked in construction, and their four children.

"I'm a down-to-earth person," says Lynne. "I never considered the possibility of seeing a ghost. I had never thought about it. It was the last thing on my mind when we moved into this house."

First, her children told her that something was wrong with the house in Fairbury. Her daughter Michelle reported hearing a voice and being shaken while she was in bed. "I didn't think much about it at first," says Lynne. "Children have vivid imaginations. I made excuses and had a million theories why it could have happened."

Then her oldest daughter, 12-year-old Deanna, saw a full-bodied, misty apparition that passed through her bedroom. It was the apparition of a man wearing a slouch hat, a stiff flannel shirt, and boots.

"I don't know whether that was the straw that broke the camel's back," says Lynne. "She had seen so many things, including having something hold her down in the bed. Deanna is very smart and articulate. So I didn't know what to think. We knew we were experiencing something."

Then, while she was folding sheets and towels and putting them into the linen closet, Lynne saw a full-bodied apparition herself. "I didn't know what it was called, a shadow man," says Lynne. "I didn't know what it was. I was terrified. It had dimension, like seeing a real person."

After Lynne and her husband separated, then became divorced, Deanna had the most terrifying experience of all. At three a.m., she ran down the stairs and into her mother's bedroom. She told her mother that something had awakened her, and refused to go back to her room. That night she stayed in her mother's room.

"That was a month before we called DIEPART," says Lynne. "By the time they came, I called it a paranormal party. Each of my children were having experiences. So was I. I didn't know what to think."

After her husband left, and later died, the paranormal incidents increased. Objects disappeared. Lynne put scissors in a drawer, only to find them in the bedroom. Her keys were moved from the kitchen to the living room.

Then she felt a tap on her shoulder. No one was there. By this point, Lynne was averaging only an hour or two of sleep a night.

"I was cursing the blue moon," says Lynne. "I was so mad. I got shoved down the railing. Shoved down on the bed. I'd see things out of the corner of my eye. I'd turn and there was nothing there. I'd see someone leaning over my bed and disappear. I saw shadow men. So did my children."

When DIEPART showed up in June of 2005, the activity lessened. "When DIEPART does an investigation, they don't usually tell the client what's going on," says Lynne. "I finally could get some sleep—I got about five hours a night."

She was unaware that the DIEPART team members were being assaulted by the paranormal while they did their investigation. Everyone had experiences. The team saw a full-bodied apparition cross the upstairs hallway and disappear into the wall. Then they looked up and watched an orb float on the ceiling of the living room.

Lynne, who had seen the orb herself, was relieved to have the paranormal investigators as fellow witnesses to the strange occurrences she had experienced.

"You can't tell everyone you know you're seeing these things," says Lynne. "People will think you're crazy. You can't talk to your colleagues at work about it. You can't tell them how the table levitated the night before. But the DIEPART team understands."

Lynne's positive experiences with the DIEPART team motivated her to become an investigator. Part of her job is helping clients deal with the ghostly experiences they're having, letting them know they're not alone or crazy.

"You think of every natural cause for this stuff," says Lynne. "Since we have pets, I would think that the cat is going bump in the night. They jump from place to place, knock things over. They get up on shelves. They break things. Every time I checked on a noise, there was nothing there. It wasn't our cat. The DIEPART team moved our pets away from the house before they did their investigation."

On numerous occasions, Lynne encountered a strange spirit in her new house in Iowa. She was surprised when the DIEPART team informed her that they believed a ghost had followed her there. "I'm hoping that most cases aren't like mine, residual hauntings. Some ghosts appear once at a certain time, like a woman in white walking down the hallway. We had interactive ghosts. They wanted to make contact with us."

Lynne learned that drug addicts had lived in the Fairbury house for many years. Many people had died of overdoses there in terrible circumstances. The house had a heaviness about it of sadness and grief from the broken lives of the addicts. When she moved to Des Moines after splitting up with her husband, Lynne never expected that one of ghosts would follow her. Only this time, she had to face the ghosts alone with her four children.

"I couldn't believe it was happening again," says Lynne.

Determined not to suffer the way she had in Fairbury, she went on the offensive in Des Moines. "I started studying everything I could, investigating, trying to figure it out. You'd be amazed at how much I learned. Investigating other people's hauntings helped me, too. It furthered my understanding of what had happened to me and my family. I was a support system for them, and they were one for me. It was terrible in Fairbury, but I found that I could bring it down to just a nuisance. The biggest thing someone can do is just get on with their life."

Lynne has discovered that the ghost mimics people. "When I'm with my family, they'll say they've seen me when I haven't been there. I looked in the mirror and saw my fiancé Scott, when he wasn't there."

Lynne's fiancé, Scott, is also a DIEPART team member, and now her daughter Deanna has become a paranormal investigator as well. "She's a lot like me. She's a junior paranormal expert."

Lynne takes her investigations seriously, even when she's a patient at a hospital. Lynne was admitted to the nineteenth-century vintage Boone County Hospital for a gastric problem recently. Unlike other patients who stay in their rooms, she and her fiancé got a private tour of the morgue in the basement of the old hospital.

"The nurses had seen apparitions. So we took our equipment down there to do readings," says Lynne. "Iowa has a history of hauntings. There are tons of coal mines and lots of cave-ins. It's a spooky place."

But now Lynne and her family aren't spooked. "It takes a lot to rattle my kids," she says.

Spirits in the Darkness

Four hours away from Des Moines is the Cherokee House, a 1918 two-story farmhouse on 240 acres of land. On the vast countryside, the wind whips around the barn and fences and through the grass and makes the walls of the farmhouse shake. Often, people mistake the sound of the wind for ghosts.

Ed's was the second family to live in this house. He and his family moved in more than 30 years ago, when Ed was seven or eight. It is the house where Ed's first wife, Jane, died of cancer in 1994. Today he lives there with his second wife, Judy. They've been together for nearly a decade.

Ed was no stranger to the paranormal. He had his first experience at the age of 15 when he was alone in the house. He was standing in the kitchen looking out the window. Then he heard the pattering sound of footsteps get louder. He ran through the room, thinking that his mother had returned from the grocery store. But she wasn't there.

At the age of 27, Ed had another paranormal experience. One morning, he had gotten up early to do the chores that he did every day. When he got tired, about noon, he took a 15-minute nap before returning to work. He leaned back on the wall of the living room to sleep, but the sound of a bowling ball rolling down the upstairs hallway awakened him. He stood up and heard bells tinkling. He wasn't certain at first whether he had dreamt it. But when he heard the sound again, he knew it wasn't a dream.

He ran upstairs and discovered that nothing had fallen from the walls. Ed shook his head. He couldn't explain what had happened.

Just two days later, his wife Judy walked into the kitchen while Ed was asleep in the bedroom. All the lights were on. "Ed," she cried. "Didn't I tell you to leave the lights off when you leave?"

Still half awake, Ed approached her from the bedroom. "Honey, I turned them off."

Judy stared at him, as though she didn't believe what he had said.

Another time when Judy found some broken glass bowls on the floor, she got scared. "Ed, come here," she cried.

He came in from the outdoors and walked into the kitchen.

"Don't walk too far in," said Judy. "You'll get glass in your feet."

Ed was flabbergasted. "Who did this?"

"I don't know." Judy picked up the broom and began sweeping the glass into the dust pan.

Another time, when Judy was upstairs cleaning, she noticed that the photograph of Ed's first wife was tossed on the floor, face down. She picked it up and put it back on the wall. Then it fell down again. She noticed that the hook had fallen out. She hammered it back in. Then she picked the photo up and put it back on the wall.

Because of the unseen guests, the once well-kept farm became disorganized. Farm equipment that weighed thousands of pounds moved on its own. Ed went out one morning to use the thresher and discovered it had been moved. Some of the equipment in the shed had been turned on. Then when he went into the barn, he found that thick rope was hanging from the upper hay barn, looped over a beam 15 feet high. It dangled three feet above the hay floor. Ed didn't have a ladder that would reach that high. There was no means to get it over the beam. Who had put it up there?

Ed's daughter, who lived in Colorado, visited an Indian psychic to ask about their problems with the house. The psychic said there was an evil spirit roaming around, moving inside and outside of the house, draining Ed and Judy of their energy and health, and that the house was too dangerous for them to live in. So the couple called team DIEPART for help on September 10, 2005.

Joe and the team met at a Walmart in Des Moines and drove four hours to the Cherokee House. The night was clear. There was a steady wind that blew through the vast countryside.

Once Ed had told Joe the history of the house, the team discussed places to set up its detection equipment. There was a lot of area to cover. They decided to set EVP and EMP equipment throughout the farmhouse. The tape recorders would only catch the sounds of the wind in the barn, since it was so old; so the team decided to use controlled experiments, instead.

Motion detectors were placed in the hay barn. DIEPART team member Lisa set up a tape recorder in one of the machine sheds, where there'd be no interference from the wind.

The team set up the controlled experiments in the basement and on the main floor. Pennies were placed on the washer and dryer. Since no one was around, the movement of the coins revealed ghostly presences.

Upstairs, in the hallway where Ed had heard the bowling ball roll on the floor, Joe set up paint spray cans. He put motion detectors in the bedrooms with digital video recorders.

The team did a walk-through before they turned out the lights.

It was a dark night, but the sky was so clear they could see the constellations. Team members Lisa and Theresa brought their cameras outside. Suddenly, Lisa, who was recording, stepped back and nudged her friend. The two watched a couple of orbs hovering above the trees on the east side of the tool shed. They were the shape of beach balls, glowing over the trees.

They followed the orbs as they bounced around the farm, one by one, then disappeared into the shadows.

The team concluded that the ghosts that inhabited the farmhouse were friendly ones. That was fine with Ed and Judy. They could endure breaking glasses and unexplained noises. They planned to live there with the ghosts as long as they could.

Call Me Peanut

COLFAX, IOWA
NAMES FICTIONALIZED

Three families have lived in this two-story farmhouse since it was built in the mid-nineteenth century. It's a forbidding place with lots of rooms and hidden nooks and crannies. The first floor has over six rooms, and the upstairs has four bedrooms and a nursery. The farmhouse has a long history of owners and hauntings.

Thomas Mitchell, who originally owned the 130-acre farm, purchased the land in 1852 from bootleggers who had driven the Sac-and-Fox Indians off the land.

Mitchell, the first settler in the county, got along with the Indians. He tried to undo the damage the bootleggers had done. He reimbursed the Indians for their land and allowed them to continue living on a section of it. In 1850, he started the town of Mitchellville when he learned that a railroad was coming through. In 1878, Mitchell became a state senator.

During the Civil War years, Mitchell hid runaway slaves in the basement, which was a serious crime. The farmhouse has lots of secret closets and rooms.

After Mitchell died at the turn of the century, the Alexander Fields family moved into the farmhouse. Fields and his wife and sister-in-law lived on the farm, and Mr. and Mrs. Fields died there. Unfortunately, the Fields and the Mitchell children fought over the property for years. For five years, one of the Fields daughters, Maggie, sued the Mitchells to get control of the property. She failed, dying soon afterward.

The ownership of the farmhouse changed again early in 2005 when the May family moved in. From the moment they unpacked their belongings, their scary experiences began.

One night, when the other children were asleep, David May was awakened by an apparition who called him "Peanut." No one had ever called David "Peanut." The wheat-colored apparition sat on his bed and held out his hand to the boy. When David reached out to touch it, it disappeared. Amazingly, David wasn't scared by what he had seen. He told his parents the ghost was friendly, like Casper.

His mother, Wendy May, soon saw something strange: a full-bodied apparition of a woman dressed in 1970s clothing. Mrs. May believed that the ghost was a family member who had lived in their house.

Not long after that, Mrs. May was puzzled when she couldn't find her sapphire ring. Every night, she placed it on the night stand. Two days later, she found it on the dining room table. Had the ghost she had seen moved it? She found a nineteenth-century silver box on a table. She had never seen one in the house before. Where was it from?

The unexplained incidents increased. Knockings and rappings scared the children. They'd run up the stairs and find that no one was there. Locked doors would open and shut.

By the time team DIEPART came in April of 2006, the Mays had had enough of their ghostly experiences. Just as Joe was setting up equipment there, he heard something strange.

"I heard a voice," says Joe. "I turned around. Who could have said it? I listened to the recording and heard a voice say, 'Maggie.'"

Maggie was the Fields daughter who had fought for the ownership of the house. Maybe the silver box was hers. Was she showing the Mays that the house was still hers? That she never intended to leave it?

Angry Spirits

DES MOINES, IOWA
NAMES FICTIONALIZED

People talk about spirits that help them through their hard times, spirits that protect their children and their pets. Not all ghosts are kind, however; some are angry and unforgiving. There was a ghost like that at the Granger house, a small two-story wooden structure in Des Moines.

The family that lived in the Granger house couldn't ignore their angry guest. Once, the father, Pedro Lorca (not his real name), came home from work to find balls of light shooting down at him from the window. The green and white balls floated around him, then exploded into one another. Pedro yelled and ran out of the room. By the time he returned, the balls had disappeared.

That incident wasn't the beginning of the Lorcas' problems. The two boys told their parents they had seen a ghost. "Daddy," said Jose. "The ghost said hi to me."

His father touched the boy's head to reassure him. "The ghost is gone now. Far away from here."

But the ghosts were still around. Cool breezes sometimes swept through the room, lowering the temperature by as much as 20 degrees. The upstairs bedroom was cold one moment, then warm the next. Pedro began wearing his jacket inside, he was so cold.

His hands shaking, he called the DIEPART team. On May 21, 2005, Joe called in three sensitives to investigate the Lorca home. (A sensitive is a person with psychic abilities.)

LeeAnne, one of the sensitives, told Joe that she felt oppressiveness at the top of the stairs. When she climbed the stairs, she found she could go no farther than the eighth stair. As she walked through the house, LeeAnne found that the west storage room was so hot that it was difficult for her to breathe. She gasped for air and finally left the room. She walked a few steps farther into the TV room. There she felt lighter, as though a spirit was welcoming her.

But as LeeAnne walked down to the basement, she felt the oppressiveness once more. By the time she got to the pool table area, the room had become very cold. She felt a presence in the child's bedroom, an angry spirit.

After the walk-through, the DIEPART team was ready to use their instruments. They separated into smaller groups so that several members were on each floor. LeeAnne was upstairs with Jessica. Debbie was downstairs with Scott. Marianne stayed on the main floor. She turned off all the kitchen lights and turned on the recorder.

Joe placed Mylar strips on the ceiling of the basement. While he set up the equipment, he made sure that the family members who had attracted the apparitions were there.

Joe clicked on his camera. It wouldn't work, though he had recharged it the night before. He found that the batteries were dead. Scott also found that the batteries to his recorder were dead. What could have caused it?

When Joe tried to put new batteries in his camera, the batteries lifted out of his hands and flew into the air and then fell. He picked the batteries off the floor and put them in the camera. He began taking pictures.

Meanwhile, the team turned off all the lights and switched to night vision. They took their recordings. Joe later discovered he had collected a number of EVPs. Some of the voices sounded angry.

"My theory was that the Lorcas had been messing around with Ouija boards," says Joe. "They had no problems before they used one. When people use Ouija boards, they ask it open-ended questions, trying to get a response. They don't know that they're using the Ouija board to conjure spirits. It's not like asking a question in a tape recorder. Instead it's like a witch conjuring spirits over a cauldron. It's like opening up a response from the paranormal. It's similar to what happens when you feed a cat. The cat starts paying attention to you. Then the cat expects to be fed by you. Playing with a Ouija board is like opening up Pandora's Box."

Taking Joe's advice, the Lorcas put their Ouija board on the shelf. Eventually, the ghostly activity ceased.

Voices in the House

DES MOINES, IOWA

When the Smith family rented a nine-room wood frame house in northwest Des Moines, they had no idea that their lives would be changed. They soon discovered that the house had had many owners, some of them not so savory.

Soon after they moved in, the children told their parents they heard voices. When David walked into the parlor, he heard a music box playing, though there wasn't a music box in sight. He ran out of there.

One morning during the summer of 2005, Jeff, the oldest boy, heard someone whispering in the living room. He told his mother, "I can't understand what they're saying." His mother didn't believe him at all. Neither did his father, until unexplained incidents started happening to them.

The children's bedroom was next door to their parents', so when the children got scared they could knock on their parents' door, something they did many nights since they had moved into the house. They often stayed in their parents' room all night.

This night appeared to be one of those nights. The voices were so loud in Jeff's ears that he couldn't concentrate on his homework. He covered his ears, trying to stop the noise. The door slammed. Then he heard knocking sounds on the walls. His mother stopped in the doorway and saw him staring into space.

"Jeff, why aren't you doing your homework?"

"I can't hear anything. The noise is too loud."

Jeff's mother hugged him reassuringly. "You can study in our bedroom now."

"Mother, I don't want to live here anymore."

His mother looked into his eyes and said, "Don't worry, honey. We'll find a solution."

Before the DIEPART team visited them on August 17, 2005, Joe had researched the history of the house. The original owner had built it nearly a century ago, when the neighborhood was a good one. Then it went downhill and became gang-ridden. The house had many occupants over the years. Very few people stayed there very long.

Joe discovered something very strange—the EMF readings were dangerously high. What could be causing it?

"In a normal house, you have to put the EMF meter beside a radiation source even to get a reading," says Joe. "The instruments in this house were giving off-the-chart readings. We'd never seen anything like that before!"

Then the team walked out of the house, through the neighborhood, and got the same high readings. "These were dangerously high levels of radiation endangering the people who lived here," says Joe. "An ungrounded pole can cause readings like this." So the team called the power company. Once that problem was resolved, the team continued their investigation.

Though they found no photographic evidence initially, the team found evidence of paranormal activity. Kevin and Joe spent a lot of time in the basement, which had areas of cold and warmth. Within six minutes of digital audio recording, they captured 100 EVPs.

"We'd never seen anything like that!" says Joe.

When they played back the tape, they heard the voices of a white man, a black man and woman, a Latino, and little children. Why were these people at this house?

During the investigation, Mrs. Smith's toilet had backed up. When the plumber came, he cleaned out the pipes and discovered a mound of plastic bags, syringes, and other drug paraphernalia. The house had been a crack house that had been raided many times by the police.

No place has more emotion than a crack house.

"Strong emotion is often the cause of hauntings," says Shannon. "There were probably drug overdoses here. Those kinds of emotional states don't just disappear."

And indeed, they didn't; the Smiths continued to be plagued by the ghosts until they moved out a year ago.

The Stearns Haunting

LADY AMBER INN AND STEARNS MANSION
GARDEN GROVE, IOWA

The ten-bedroom Lady Amber Inn is red brick, simply built in a Grecian style. It was built in 1840 by C.S. Stearns, a wealthy merchant who lived in Garden Grove, and it later became a stop on the stagecoach line.

Located in southern Iowa, Garden Grove became a boom town when the railroad came through. The Stearns family became wealthy by investing in the Southern Pacific Railroad. In fact, one of the tracks runs right behind the mansion they built a block from the inn.

He named the inn after his racehorse, Lady Amber. The rounded pillars that surround it look foreboding, warning visitors of the horrible things that have happened there.

The mansion was the most expansive of its time, a showplace for the Stearns family. Mrs. Stearns bought heartwood pine for the floors, slate for the roof, and other rare items. The house was one of the first its kind in the nineteenth-century to have plumbing and electricity.

After 1900, the owners turned it into a brothel for soldiers who came into town. Later, it was a nursing home; many of the patients and staff heard footsteps when no one was there. Then the owners closed it down for good.

"It's not fit for habitation now," says Joe. "It'll take a lot to get it up to snuff."

The former owner of the inn and the mansion, Jennifer Rice, became a member of DIEPART because of her paranormal experiences there. (She's moved to Texas now, but her experiences are fresh in her mind.) Jennifer's experiences began when she and her husband started renovating the mansion. She had difficulty keeping workers; many of them refused to work, having seen dark shadows or heard footsteps.

"The hotel had lots of unexplained incidents," says Jennifer. "I heard stories from people about it. It was an old place with lots of cobwebs. Some of the windows were busted up. Stearns owned it in 1929, then donated it to the city when he died. The city used it as a firehouse."

When Jennifer's family, including a seven-year-old son and two daughters, ages 14 and 10, moved into the 7,500-square-foot Victorian mansion, strange things started happening immediately.

"Often, I'd stay up late working because the house was quiet and the kids were asleep. I was in the office on the northwest corner of the second floor by the stairs," says Jennifer. "I was writing a grant, when I heard footsteps coming up the stairs. I couldn't tell where the sound was coming from. I just heard the footsteps getting closer. My door was close to the stairs, so I could have seen someone coming up there. I looked out, and there was no one there."

Her husband was away on a business trip. When he returned several months later, he witnessed some unusual incidents. "He didn't believe in ghosts. Neither did I."

One day when he came home, he looked up and saw a woman standing in the window. "She was standing there, as real as could be. She stared at him. He ran upstairs to find her. There was no one there. He freaked out."

After that, her husband was more open-minded about his family's ghostly tales. Who was that woman in the window? Was it Mrs. Stearns?

Her daughter Deanna heard footsteps while she was walking in the hallway. She stopped to see whether someone was following her. She looked behind her. No one was there. "It scared the crap out of her," says Jennifer.

Deanna and Jennifer made all kinds of excuses for the paranormal events they witnessed. They talked to each other about the strange feelings they had while living there. They felt uncomfortable, as if sensing that they weren't alone.

One night, after guests she'd been entertaining had left, Jennifer heard a loud voice on the second floor. At first, she thought it was a guest who had been left behind, so she went upstairs to check. No one was there.

While she was upstairs, she made up a bed for her mother, who was coming to visit in a couple of days to attend the graduation of Jennifer's daughter Amanda. After a few days of staying with them, her mother told her she didn't want to sleep in the room, or even stay with them for Amanda's graduation. Her mother later told Jennifer the reason for her sudden desire to flee.

"My mother said she had seen a presence in the room. A woman in a white robe," says Jennifer. "She told me she wanted to stay in a hotel."

The next morning when Jennifer was out on the front porch, she saw their dog fly out of the third-floor window near the attic and land right in front of her. The dog, which was pregnant, landed on all fours and didn't lose a puppy. It was as if the dog had been carried down on a current of air safely to the ground—the dog even had to make a hard right turn away from the roof to land that way on the porch.

"It was like the dog was carefully placed on the front porch," says Jennifer. "The kids were stunned."

On June 11, 2005, Jennifer called in the DIEPART team; they investigated the mansion for three days. During their stay, they recorded a number of AVPs. In fact, the Rice family found messages on their answering machine that said, "Get out!"

While DIEPART completed their investigation, Jennifer's son was awakened by a strange force and saw a red-eyed creature in his closet. The creature shouted at him to get out of the room, and he wasted no time in complying.

A team member took a picture of a shadow man in the back yard of the inn. The man was dressed in knickers and a brown hat, not contemporary clothing.

Before she saw the photo, Jennifer had heard the story of the shadow man from an old-timer in Garden Grove. During World War I, a soldier wanted to marry one of the brothel's working girls, but his father refused to permit it. The soldier vowed to return to his beloved. Then he disappeared forever, dying in the war.

"I think we may have caught the legend," says Jennifer.

Caught on Tape

DES MOINES, IOWA

Church services can be pretty dull, but the congregation at the Danish Lutheran Church will never forget the visitor who upset one memorable service the Saturday night before Easter in 2006. While their pastor was speaking, he and his congregation heard a disembodied voice.

Just as the pastor said, "'Go in peace, 'saith the Lord," a voice came through the speakers, drowning out his words. The disembodied voice spoke in a foreign language. The strange incident was caught on video tape.

The wooden church, which was built in 1918, was undergoing renovation. These remodeling projects increased paranormal incidents, and it seemed as though each incident was connected to a new improvement. While new thermal windows were added to the upstairs atrium, a construction worker reported seeing an apparition hovering over the podium. He refused to return to his job.

The pastor and his congregation wanted to find out more about the source of the paranormal incidents they had experienced, so they called the DIEPART team. The team broke up into three groups to cover different areas of the church. Each group placed digital recorders in strategic spots where members of the congregation had reported seeing apparitions. They soon discovered that their batteries in their recorders went dead, an indication that there was paranormal activity nearby. Then an EMF meter that was placed in the choir loft started beeping, but the team members saw nothing.

The team doesn't know the language the disembodied voice spoke. They believe it could be an ancient form of Danish. But they know that the spirit is friendly. Their investigations at the church continue.

The Ghost Child Says, "Thank You"

BURLINGTON, IOWA
NAMES FICTIONALIZED

Today Megan often tells her friends what happened to her in the old house. She can't believe her own stories. But they're true.

When Megan was a young divorced mother in the winter of 2005, she moved into a big, hundred-year-old house in Burlington with her baby daughter, Mary. From the moment they moved in, she lived in fear. She wasn't the only one who experienced unexplainable events; her fiancé, Jerry, did too.

Once when she was in the baby's room feeding her daughter, Megan heard heavy breathing over the nursery monitor. The door slammed behind her; it had been left wide open and there was no way it could have closed on its own. She clutched the baby in her arms protectively, wondering what to do next.

She tried not to let her fear get the better of her until she smelled a musty odor and noticed that there were warm and cold spots. One day when Jerry was visiting her, he found the alarm clock far away from the bedside table where it was usually placed. He picked it up from the floor and put it back in its place, only to find it missing again. When he was downstairs, he watched a window screen move by itself. He heard voices he couldn't explain. The next time he saw Megan, he grabbed her shoulder. A look of fear overcame him.

"Honey, what's wrong?" asked Megan.

"I heard a child's voice say, 'Thank you,'" he told her.

Megan's eyes were wide. She wondered whether Mary was in danger every time she left her alone in the nursery. She moved the baby's crib into her bedroom.

Megan's most frightening experience was yet to come. When she was asleep the next night, she woke up suddenly. The room was dark, with only the glow of the moon lighting it. In the half light, she saw someone leaning over her. The ghost looked like a "grumpy farmer" with a drawn face. He wore blue jeans and an old shirt. She awakened Jerry just as the apparition disappeared.

"What's wrong?" Jerry grumbled.

Megan stammered. "A ghost…"

Jerry pulled the covers off and got up.

"Get Mary," sobbed Megan. "Hurry."

Jerry took Mary out of the crib. He carried the baby downstairs, where they could find a place to sleep in the living room.

After that incident, Megan realized she couldn't protect her baby in the house. When she discovered she was pregnant again, she decided that the house wasn't safe for children, so she called the DIEPART team on October 20, 2005.

Joe and the other team members came to the house to talk with Megan and Jerry. Megan was still upset about what she had seen, though the house was quiet. She felt as if she couldn't leave the baby alone. The team reassured her that they would be able to resolve the problem. By one a.m., the team began their investigation. They turned off the lights so the house was inky dark, and set up their equipment.

The upstairs master bedroom where Megan had seen the apparition was colder than the other rooms, so they put digital recorders and cameras there. While they set up their equipment, they smelled the musty odor, which was spreading through all the rooms.

Everything was quiet for 40 minutes while the team waited. The shadows flickered in the room. Suddenly a squeaking noise filled the air. Megan and several DIEPART team members went outside to see if the noise came from a moving branch. Though there was no breeze, inside the curtains were moving. The team photographed everything. When the digital photo was viewed on the computer, a green, glowing spot appeared.

A tapping sound erupted from underneath the floor of the master bedroom. Was the ghost trying to contact them?

The house seemed alive, though everyone was asleep except the DIEPART team. Since the ghost had made the tapping sound, Joe decided to encourage its response. So the team began the mental conjuring experiment. "In a mental conjuring experiment," says Joe, "one team member speaks out loud and serves as a control by reciting anything, like the alphabet or a hymn, while the rest of the team concentrates and tries to put their thoughts on one question. Who is in the house?"

As the team conjured, a crackling sound came from the master bedroom. It resembled a man's voice. But the sounds didn't show up on the audio tape. Was the man that Megan saw sitting on her bed responding to their mental conjuring experiment?

The other data the DIEPART team collected confirmed the existence of a ghostly presence. Megan and Jerry had had their fill of encountering apparitions. For the safety of the children, they moved to a new apartment.

Old Settler's Cemetery

The Old Settler's Cemetery seems to appear out of nowhere as you approach the crossroads of four streets in West Des Moines, Iowa. Built in the 1840s, the cemetery has only about a dozen graves sitting in what appears to be the middle of the road, protected only by a metal fence. The wind whips the branches of two lonely trees. It's a desolate place that few people ever visit.

"I've never seen a cemetery like this," said Joe, who came there on an investigation in the winter of 2007. "Never one with graves practically out in the middle of the street."

The DIEPART team brought several pieces of equipment with them, including a digital recorder and a Vivitar camera. They gathered a lot of EVPs, but they didn't catch any apparitions on film.

At night, visitors often see ghosts floating over the graves. The wind howls so much that it sounds like the voice of a human being. The moonlight soaks the headstones and makes them glow in the dark. Most people who visit don't stay very long.

The Laughing Ghost

OSKALOOSA, IOWA
NAMES FICTIONALIZED

Oskaloosa is a small town south of Des Moines. Shortly after this house was built in 1860, its first owner, Frederic Knight Logan, a musician, often sat on the porch and composed songs. He died there. The townsfolk think that he haunts the house. Most recently, the Oskaloosa newspaper documented the five-year story of one family's encounter with the supernatural.

In 2002, when the Jones family first moved in, they had horrifying experiences there. Every member of the family had nightmares, insomnia, and other sleeping problems. In the darkened parlor one evening, the Jones children heard disembodied voices. James, the oldest one, held his young sister's hand tightly. She screamed out in terror. She ran up the staircase with James at her heels.

"The kids are imagining stuff," Bill Jones told his wife, Eleanor.

"Bill, I've seen it too."

Only that morning, her hair dryer had disappeared; she later discovered it lying on the comforter in their bedroom. When she went into the bathroom, the tub was filled with water.

"Maybe James played a practical joke," Bill offered.

"He wouldn't do anything like that."

But later, as Bill watched the gas stove turn on by itself, he realized that his family was telling the truth. Just as he turned the flame off, he saw the apparition of a man hovering over the cabinets. He ran to the image, and it disappeared.

A day later, Eleanor and James watched a female apparition climb the stairs. The sandy-colored ghost was dressed in nineteenth-century clothing, lifting her long blue dress as she walked. By the time she got to the top of the stairs, she had disappeared.

Rumors about the ghost spread through Oskaloosa. When the DIEPART team began their investigation in May of 2006, the *Oskaloosa Herald* sent a reporter to cover the event. But he left before the investigation began at 10:30 p.m. He wasn't prepared to stay up all night.

The team had hardly begun their observations when a man's loud, raspy laugh rippled through the upstairs and echoed in the hallway. Then one of the EMF meters the team had set up in the hall went off.

And that wasn't the end of it. The kitchen filled with the overpowering smell of lilacs, and the other team members smelled it throughout the house. A moment later, there was a long, bellowing sound. It was as if Frederic Logan was playing his trombone.

"Having a death in a place isn't a prerequisite of having hauntings," says Joe. "It could be the musician who is haunting the house. But it could also be someone else. People believe that a haunting occurs along with a tragic event. That's not always the case."

Joe tells his clients that ghosts aren't limited to the technology of their age. From 1984 to 1986, there was a documented case in Doddleston, England, of a sixteenth-century ghost named Thomas Harden using the computer to send messages. While Debbie and Ken Webster were out of the house, Harden left over 50 messages, which used pre-Shakespearean sentence construction. "The ghost left messages, when the computer wasn't hooked up to the Internet or even turned on," says Joe. "Manipulation of objects is commonplace when there's a haunting."

Before the team packed up in the morning, Joe saw a dark shadow by the back hall entrance near the dining room. The shadow seemed to be heading for him, then suddenly veered to the left. It passed within several millimeters of his feet. Then it vanished.

Was the apparition the ghost of Frederic Logan?

Where's the Ghost?

PUTNAM MUSEUM
DAVENPORT, IOWA

The Putnam Museum in Davenport is a scary place. It's loaded with cases of Egyptian mummies, some of which are open, revealing 2,000-year-old leather-skinned bodies wrapped in discolored linen.

Spooked staff members, who believe the museum is haunted, called in the DIEPART team to investigate before Halloween 2007. This was the first time the team had investigated a museum.

Marketing intern Nick Edwards and Lori Arguello, a media relations assistant, brought in the team for the Halloween event called "Haunted Hill," which was scheduled for October 26, 2007.

Arguello told reporter Kay Luna that the mummies had just undergone CAT scans. So bringing in the DIEPART team was just going "one step further."

Joe brought in his parabolic microphones to record EVPs. The museum was quiet as the DIEPART team set up their equipment, recording audio and video throughout the night.

After they reviewed the tape, they did find some EVPs in the Egyptian Gallery. One was a recording of a woman giggling. Another voice said, "Anna."

Kent Amerine, DIEPART team member, told reporters that they didn't have enough evidence to conclude that the museum was haunted. Though there is a chance the sound of the woman's voice could be caused by a spirit, it's more likely that the EVP comes from the barrage of electromagnetic signals that surrounds us. It could also be caused by a conversation in another room that the microphone picked up.

Though no one can prove the museum is haunted, everyone agrees that the new Egypt exhibit is enough to scare people. The sight of the decapitated head of a mummy as visitors enter the exhibit sends many people out the door.

Stumped by a Ghost

NAMES FICTIONALIZED

Kellie Wilmot has had more than her fair share of encounters with ghosts in her 41 years. Based in Sioux City, Iowa, Kellie has been DIEPART team regional manager for three years. By day a production manager at Sue Bee Honey, at night she investigates paranormal activity in her area. Her most astounding case is that of the 12-room Richardson house. Though the 1910 vintage house looks like others, it is not.

It was home to the Richardson family—father, mother, and four children, including twins Julie and Cindy. Kellie first heard the three-year-old Cindy talk about Sally, the ghost child she had seen. Sally had asked Cindy for three dollars. Cindy played with Sally all day.

"I thought that was strange," says Kellie. "How does a three-year-old know anything about money?"

Mrs. Richardson told Kellie she was scared because Cindy said that Sally had crawled into bed with her. Cindy didn't appear to be upset, however; she believed that Sally was her friend. After Cindy's bed was made in the morning, it became crumpled and unkempt during the day. The sheets were wrinkled and damp. Was Sally doing it?

The Sioux City, Iowa, Paranormal Advanced Research Team (SCIPART) investigation began with a bang. Noises flowed out from the walls of the house. Team members could hear voices when no one was around. And when one member of the SCIPART team, John, walked through hot spots of the house, he felt someone touch his shirt. He looked around, and there was no one behind him. A moment later, it happened again.

After the lights had been turned off, John sat on the bed in Cindy's upstairs bedroom. A Raggedy Ann doll was seated across from him on a shelf. A little while later, he looked at the doll again and noticed that it had moved ten inches in the course of 20 minutes. Suddenly, he felt something sharp strike his back. He looked behind him and saw the foot of the doll in his back.

"We tried to debunk it," says Kellie. "We tried moving the bedspread to see if that would affect the doll. It didn't. Then we tried shaking the bed. That didn't affect the doll either. It would have had to be something like a car going by rattling the whole room. This 12-room house is in a rural area, away from highways and roads."

The video from their infrared camera showed the doll move, almost floating down onto the bed. Later that evening, when another investigator was sitting on the bed, his radio flew out of his hands and landed two feet in front of him. The team also saw a number of orbs on the film.

"I tell my investigators, it's not the dead you have to fear, it's the living," says Kellie. "Something happened at the Richardson house that proved my point. When I was upstairs and my eyes hadn't gotten used to the dark, I squatted down to look at the hallway where one of my investigators had seen shadows running between the rooms. Suddenly I felt a tug on my leg and someone breathing in my ear. I was about to scream when I saw it was Julie, Cindy's twin sister. She had come upstairs to go to bed. She scared the hell out of me."

Two weeks later, the team got another phone call from the Richardsons. The girls were waking up in the middle of the night screaming. Cindy had seen a full-bodied apparition of the little girl. Cindy's bed started shaking so much it had awakened her in the middle of the night.

The team focused their attention on Cindy's bedroom. They found that the temperature dropped 30 or 40 degrees there. The cold spot would travel from her bed across the room and into the closet. The team also got some strong EVPs, which mentioned another ghost named Jessica.

"After researching the history of the house, we found that a family had lived there at the turn of the century," says Kellie. "But we couldn't get any details about them because the assessor's office only lists the number of occupants."

The team investigated the Richardson house for three nights. On the third night, they saw the full-bodied apparition of the little girl that appeared like a mist.

"It was glittery and smoky," says Kellie. "The apparition started to rise three or four feet off the ground. It came between John and me. We started snapping pictures. Then it was gone."

Was that apparition the ghost of Sally? Did she move the doll on Cindy's bed? The sleepless nights continue at the Richardson house. No matter how they try, they can't stop seeing ghosts.

House of the Paranormal

JEFFERSON, IOWA

How can a mobile over a child's playpen start spinning on its own? There was no open window, no way could a breeze get into that room. And yet every member of team DIEPART saw the mobile spin during their investigation of the "Spinner House."

The three-story house, which was built in 1913, is located in an isolated place in rural central Iowa. Neighbors are so far away you have to travel miles to find them. All around the house are fields of corn and grass where the wind blows relentlessly day after day.

Over the past 30 years, several families have lived there. Today one family—Tom, an Army lieutenant, his wife, Jane, and their three children—have lived there for a year and a half in fear. They wished the uninvited spirits would leave them alone. Some nights they were up all night, listening to the constant rapping on the walls. They believed they could keep the spirits out just by closing the door of their bedroom, but even with the door closed, Jane saw an apparition hovering over her bed. Jane and Tom didn't want to scare their children, so they kept what they had seen secret.

They were unaware that everyone in this family of five had seen an apparition. The youngest daughter, who was just a toddler, had seen a man in the green room in the basement. Her dog wouldn't sleep in the room. Her mother saw the apparition peering into the children's bedrooms. At night, the dogs barked at shadows.

Then, during the early 1990s, while Tom was fighting in Iraq, Jane and her children were left alone in the house. As if that wouldn't have been stressful enough, while Tom was gone the noises got worse. Doors banged shut and opened on their own. The lights went on and off without anyone touching them.

Jane shook when she saw a full-bodied apparition of a man at three in the morning. The man sat down on her bed and faced her. At first she could not speak. Then she recovered her senses and screamed, at which the apparition disappeared.

Another day, while the family was out of the house, the bathtub filled up with water and overflowed. When Jane returned, the water had poured through the floor, ruining the floors and the tile downstairs. As Jane stood sobbing over the damage, several books rose into the air and flew above her head. She screamed. She had had enough of this ghost. She needed help.

So Jane called team DIEPART on August 7, 2005. Joe Leto scheduled the investigations from 11:20 p.m. to 4:30 a.m. Jane made sure that the dogs were kept in a separate area so they wouldn't disturb the investigation.

While they were setting up their equipment, the team witnessed unexplained events. "We saw objects move. Baby toys moved on their own," says Joe.

As they walked through the room, they felt the temperature drop. The air was heavy. But the event that surprised the DIEPART team was watching that mobile spin on its own in the attic.

"I'd never seen anything like that," says Joe. "We tried to debunk it. We couldn't. We tried to duplicate the mobile spinning by walking past it again and again. It didn't work."

Downstairs the living room grew colder. The team members put on their jackets, though it was summertime.

Joe started asking questions about the house. He contacted the Langhorn family, who had lived in the house previously. "We discovered that Jimmy, the last owner's son, had committed suicide there," says Joe. "Apparently Jimmy was a practical joker. He continued his practical jokes when Jane and her family moved in. He thought that Jane was his mother. He was rapping to get her attention." Later when Jimmy's mother died, the apparitions stopped. Jimmy had moved on to the other side with his real mother.

Was Jimmy playing a practical joke when he started the mobile spinning? Maybe he just wanted to scare the DIEPART team and let them know he was boss.

The Ghosts are Nice People

NAMES FICTIONALIZED

Winterset, Iowa, hasn't changed for centuries. This rural countryside was made famous by Robert James Waller's bestselling novel, *The Bridges of Madison County*. But don't be deceived by the magic of the rolling hills and 100-year-old covered bridges. Many places in this picturesque town have been haunted, and remain so to this day.

Chris, his wife Tish, and their two children, Jennie and Sam, thought that the house they moved into in the fall of 2004 was like other places they had lived. It wasn't.

One day, before they were even unpacked, Jennie told her mother, "I saw a man and a girl. They're both nice people."

"Jennie, I'm sure our neighbors are nice," Tish replied.

"Mommie, they aren't our neighbors. They live here with us."

Tish thought her daughter had a vivid imagination. She knew they had been playing with the Ouija board. But the kids loved to play with it, and, after all, it was harmless.

Tish never gave a thought to what her daughter had said. She was busy unpacking the boxes from their move. Since the house was so large, she spent a day putting together each room. She put the rag rug on the parquet kitchen floor and filled the cabinets with dishes and pots and pans. After working all day, she was exhausted.

By the time Chris got home from work at the plant, she was in bed, asleep. He shut off the lights quietly so as not to wake her. The room was so dark, you couldn't see the windows, or the lawn outside. He quickly fell asleep.

Then they felt the bed lift into the air and move slowly back and forth, rocking like a ship. Then it moved up and down, tossing the pillows off onto the floor and throwing the coverlet down. When the bed turned sideways, Chris was thrown onto the floor. Confused by what had happened, Tish reached her arm out to his hand so that she could pull him back onto the bed. But her arm was moving so much she couldn't reach him. Then they both looked up as something ghostlike swooped down on Chris while he was on the floor.

Tish cried out. The dark apparition floated up to the ceiling and disappeared through the wall. She had never seen anything like that. Suddenly the bed stopped moving. Everything was quiet.

In the morning, Tish found herself shaking while she unpacked the vases that would be placed on tables in the living room. Chris was still asleep. He'd leave for work at noon.

She heard giggling from the upstairs bedroom, then a crash. She ran upstairs to see Jennie playing with her dolls alone. One Madame Alexander doll that was placed underneath the bed flew into the air.

"What's going on, Jennie?"

Jennie seemed unaffected by what had happened. "The girl is playing with my doll. I let her."

Tish looked around. "You mean Julie?"

Jennie shook her head. Tish and Chris had another sleepless night the next evening. Though everything seemed quiet at first, they were both awakened by a roaring sound. The bed was shifting from side to side, rolling. It raised itself a foot off the ground, then fell with a crash.

Tish started sobbing. "I'm afraid, sweetie."

Chris called in DIEPART in June of 2005.

Joe knew this would be a tough case, so he brought in six other investigators. They used three parabolic microphones, as well as six analog and digital recorders. They turned off the furnace and the HVAC system so they wouldn't get false readings.

"We picked up a dozen EVP readings in the boy's room near the desk," says Joe. "None of them were threatening in nature."

Joe attached Mylar strips to the ceiling of Jennie's room to see what would happen. Since the furnace was turned off and the windows were closed, there was no reason for the strips to move.

The cameras caught the strips moving back and forth like a pendulum.

When Joe played back the recording, something unexpected was on it. "The recording revealed a voice saying, 'The kids saw me.'"

The kids attracted something when they played with the Ouija board. "If you pay attention to a cat, the cat will sit on your lap," says Joe. "It's the same way with spirits. If you contact a spirit via a Ouija board, you're paying attention to them. They will visit you. In every case, these ghosts will follow the people from place to place everywhere they live."

Tish found herself packing everything into boxes again. They were moving. They couldn't share their beautiful Madison County house with ghosts.

Are You Done Yet?

WILTON, IOWA

Sometimes you can be surprised by a ghost. That's what happened to Stan Gaunt. Stan and his wife, Dee Dee, have been living with their young daughter in a prefabricated house on the southeastern side of Wilton for more than three years.

While he was taking a shower one morning in June 2006, Stan heard a female voice say, "Are you done yet?" At first he thought it might be his wife, Dee Dee. But soon he realized that she was gone. So was their young daughter.

Just a few days later, when Stan was ready to climb into the shower, he felt something massaging his head. He shook his head and left the room. He began to think he might be hallucinating because he was under stress at work.

A moment later, when Stan was coming through the hallway, Dee Dee heard a voice say, "Where are you going?" She also heard footsteps coming down the hallway and smelled something "fruity" in the air.

While both of her parents were wondering if they were nuts, their daughter told them that she had seen two ghosts: one was a "lady" and the other an "angel." The angel, who appeared to be a little girl, asked her daughter whether she was afraid of ghosts.

So both Dee Dee and her daughter reassured Stan that he wasn't hallucinating. He had had a paranormal experience. Though Dee Dee had always believed in ghosts, she knew that Stan never gave them a thought until he started hearing voices.

One night, Stan and Dee Dee used the Ouija board to contact the "lady" and the "angel." They placed the board on a table and placed their hands on the planchette. The board shook and rose. Then the planchette pointed out a stream of letters. Stan copied them down quickly. It was a message from a 30-year-old woman who told them there were other ghosts in their house.

Their encounter with the ghosts through the Ouija board only made their life more difficult. The voices of the "angel" and "lady" followed them through their daily activities. Stan could not sleep. He was awakened by noise every night.

In desperation, the Gaunts called in team DIEPART to investigate. Joe decided to use a number of controlled experiments. He placed golf balls on the counter by the refrigerator where the angel often hung out. In the bedroom, he put bottle caps on paper with circles drawn on them. The Gaunts had been stirring up ghostly activity by using their Ouija board. Since Joe knew that ghosts usually return to the Ouija board where they were first contacted, they put the Ouija board on the bed in the master bedroom and surrounded it with four Mylar strips.

After spending a night at the Gaunts, the DIEPART team confirmed what the family experienced. Temperatures often dropped unexplainably, a sure indication of paranormal activity. With their parabolic microphones placed strategically throughout the house, their digital recorder caught lots of voices, including one with a Southern accent saying, "I'm the one that said that."

The paranormal activity hasn't stopped for the Gaunts. Stan keeps his eyes out when he takes a shower. He hopes his shoulder won't be tapped. He turns up the spray so he can't hear the voice and wonders who the ghost is and why it's bothering him.

A Psychotherapist Who Takes Time for Ghosts

Why would a psychotherapist become a ghost hunter? "I was always interested in the paranormal," says Terri Smith, who has a Masters in Social Work degree from the University of Iowa and has been a DIEPART team member for three years. "I can't say that I had any huge paranormal experiences. I thought that there was a bubble around me. Nothing seemed to happen, though I was a believer. But when I heard the EVPs, I knew there was something there. They astounded me. On one investigation, I saw a shadow person out of the corner of my eye. I haven't seen anything levitate. I'd love to see a book fly off the shelves."

Terri helps the team debunk some of the places they investigate. Her knowledge of psychology helps her understand the difference between a hallucination and a true paranormal experience. When clients file a questionnaire about the paranormal activity, she asks them questions about their mental health history. "Schizophrenia can give someone symptoms that can appear as if someone is having paranormal experiences," says Terri. "They hear voices that aren't there. When we look at paranormal phenomena, we also look at the client psychology as well."

Terri has been on investigations where there was no scientific evidence to back up the clients' claims of the paranormal. "If we're not getting any EVPs or AVPs or any photographic evidence to back up their claims, it's probably a mental health issue," she said.

Terri observes a variety of traits to determine the possibility that mental illness could be the source of the clients' strange experiences. "We look at how they present themselves. People can have bizarre experiences with bipolar illnesses, as well. We notice how their hygiene is, whether their house is clean. Messiness can indicate depression. Just because someone is diagnosed with mental illness doesn't mean that paranormal activities aren't happening, however."

In one case Terri and the team investigated, the client faked the paranormal activity at her house. She tossed objects into the air to make them appear to levitate. Then she tapped on the walls with a hammer. "We put cameras all over the house and caught her in the act," says Terri. "There were some mental health issues going on there. It was an elaborate plan. Even her husband was unaware of it. I think I'd classify her as having more of a personality disorder—attention-seeking, dramatic, histrionic kind of behavior."

Most cases Terri investigates aren't faked. She is familiar with cases where a number of people witness the same paranormal events. She investigated one old mansion where she had worked that had been converted into an office building. While it was being renovated, residents heard strange sounds—like a baby crying when there was no baby there. The housekeepers who cleaned the offices at night refused to go to the basement. One had seen a child at the top of the stairs when no child could have been there.

While visiting the old house, says Terri, "I saw a dark translucent ball, an orb, near the chair of my client. I was so shocked I didn't say anything. I'd never seen anything like that before. When the equipment malfunctioned in that office, I knew I was witnessing a paranormal event; I wasn't the only one who saw that stuff."

At one house, Terri learned a lot about recording ghostly sounds. "I talked with another investigator about how to set up the equipment, why we put things where we did. We got lots of EVPs. I can only think that the ghosts are on some other frequency from us. We can't hear it with our naked ears. You can put out all kinds of theories. We don't know. We just collect pieces of evidence."

Though she hasn't come across any demonic spirits, Terri, who comes from a conservative Christian family, believes that ghosts can be evil. "Our group always prays for protection before we enter a client's house."

Terri lives in an old house that was built in 1927, along with five dogs and cats that she rescued from an animal shelter. Though she doesn't think her house is haunted, the animals won't go into several rooms. "It has a lot of history. A couple lived there before my husband and I did. The daughter got married there. Then the mother had a heart attack by the fireplace right before she sold the house."

"I love investigating paranormal activity," Terri says. "It's a wonderful hobby. I don't mind spending hours going through video and audio tape, even though my eyes start to cross."

Talking to a Ghost

DES MOINES, IOWA
NAMES FICTIONALIZED

Children often have imaginary friends; it's a natural part of growing up. But Casey Deaton's mother began to worry when he told her about his friend.

When Melissa heard four-year-old Casey repeating "yes" and "no" as if he were answering questions, the boy told her that he was talking to a man. Melissa looked through their kitchen window and saw that no one was there. Who was Casey talking to?

"What's he asking you?" asked Melissa.

"He's saying naughty stuff," replied Casey. At first Melissa thought that he was simply making up an imaginary friend. Casey said the friend was older. When she asked him to describe him, Casey wouldn't. She got worried after Casey told her that his "friend" was telling him to do things like murder the dog.

"Mommy, I'm afraid," cried Casey.

His mother held him tightly, trying to reassure him that everything would be all right.

While the family was out shopping, Mr. Long, a neighbor, looked out his window at their house. He fell backward in surprise. He couldn't believe what he'd seen. A man was standing in the picture window of the front room.

A day later, Casey's father, Joe, saw a shadowy figure moving from room to room. He began to believe what Casey was telling them—especially when he saw a small boy staring at him from the hallway. He chased the apparition, and suddenly it disappeared.

After a guest in their home heard an Irish brogue voice whispering in his ear, they decided to call team DIEPART in February 2005. The team arrived at 11:30 p.m. to get a tour of the house. They set up motion detectors in Casey's bedroom and took EVP readings in the dining room.

With the house dark, the team was quiet. Voices seemed to rise out of Casey's room. Everyone on the team heard them. There was whispering in the kitchen as if two children were talking. At that moment, a cold wind passed through the rooms and their equipment batteries went dead.

But the team had gathered enough evidence to verify what Casey and his father had seen. His father thought that it wasn't safe for them to stay there, and soon afterward the Deaton family moved out of the house. To this day, neither Casey nor his parents have forgotten the years they spent in the haunted house.

Vicky Was Here

NEWTON, IOWA
CASE NAMES FICTIONALIZED

How could a photo of a nameless stranger appear in a house? That's what happened in Newton, Iowa. Penny's house, a simple one story with a basement, has been the site of several investigations for the DIEPART team. Penny's young son, Sam, told her that he felt a strange, threatening presence in the basement.

Penny was uneasy about what her son had said, but assumed he was imagining things. One day, after she came from work at the hospital, she placed her keys in the usual place, on a hook in the kitchen. When she went to get them the next day, they were gone. Her keys had moved from the hook where she placed them into a cabinet.

Penny came back home from work and found that the furniture had shifted. The living room couch, which was too heavy for Sam to lift, had moved ten meters away, close to the front door. How could that have happened? When she asked Sam whether he'd seen anything, he just shook his head. The she realized that the door she had locked was now unlocked.

Objects began being moved from their customary places—even when the house was locked, when no one was there. The final straw was when Penny found a coupon and a photo of a woman with the name "Vicky" and the year "1981" written on the back. Vicky was wearing a Western checkered shirt. Who was Vicky? Penny had never met her.

Penny showed Vicky's photo to Joe on his first investigation of the house in 2006. After doing some research, Joe discovered that Vicky had been a maid at a local hotel, She had disappeared years ago.

This was no easy case for the DIEPART team. It took four visits to Penny's house to collect data. Each time they got readings that were unheard of. The EMF meter on the catwalk beeped when no one was there. Everyone heard a humming noise.

Then Joe discovered laughter on the tapes. The voices said the investigators would never find anything there. They joked about the questions the team asked Penny.

"The EVPs were making fun of us," says Joe.

Penny was upset about their discoveries. She was afraid to leave Sam alone in the house. He was awakened by all kinds of noises, and became more and more afraid. Penny decided she had had enough.

By the time the team finished their last investigation, Penny and Sam had moved out. The events they experienced have not been explained. No one has had the courage to move in there. To this day, the house remains empty.

Farmhouse at the Edge of Haunted

Dan Berger, former Regional Manager of DIEPART who now owns the ghost hunting company, became a paranormal researcher by accident.

"I've always been interested in the paranormal," says 55-year-old Berger, who is based in Des Moines. "I've always been into alternative science. I like having different ways of looking at things. I called DIEPART and joined. Here I am."

Berger and his wife lived in an old farmhouse built in the early 1900s that had "issues." Knickknacks would disappear and then reappear. One time, when Dan was going downstairs, he saw a shadow of a man walking across the floor. When he turned his head, the apparition was gone. It was so real that Dan called the police. They searched the house and found that no one was there.

In December of 2005, his wife was dying of cancer. According to Berger, a week or so before her death, weird things started to happen.

"She'd sit up in the bed, as if she was talking to someone," says Berger. "I kept telling her to lie down. This went on for two nights. She was like a puppy dog communicating to something. Then she passed."

After a year, Berger remarried to woman named Liana. They continued to live in the old farmhouse "We went to Las Vegas and picked up a bunch of knickknacks. One day when I came back from work, everything we bought was piled up in one place."

Then the most startling thing happened one morning when Dan was downstairs eating breakfast and Liana was upstairs in bed, half asleep with the bedroom door shut. According to Berger, his wife was still dreaming, but the smell of the bacon cooking awakened her. She was lying on her side with her head on the pillow. "She told me she felt someone grab her head and turn it from one side to the other," says Berger. "She yelled out 'Dan' and realized I wasn't there. I screamed back that I was downstairs frying bacon. She freaked."

Now Liana, a member of the DIEPART team, accompanies Dan on some of his investigations. The farmhouse still has unexplained events that the DIEPART team has yet to investigate. Recently, Dan lost his keys. He couldn't find them for several days. Finally, he found them upstairs in a box in the bedroom closet. When Liana's wedding ring disappeared, her ring reappeared in the same place.

One time when Liana was dying her hair in the bathroom, she left for a moment. When she returned, the dye was all over the tile. Strangely enough, the dye wasn't on any of the bath towels or the shower curtain.

• • •

One of Berger's most interesting cases concerned an old house where they took photos of orbs. "One of them looked like an ectoplasm," says Berger. He'd never seen an orb like that before. "I showed it to Joe. He'd never seen anything like it, either."

Many people have seen an older man sitting in a chair at the kitchen table. When Berger described the apparition to the woman who first owned the house, she said it was the man who lived there in the early 1900s. He just walked out of the house and disappeared. He remodeled the house himself and added an addition. On one wall, he built a long bookcase.

When the current family who lived there started remodeling, things began to happen. "Books flew off of the bookcases," says Berger. "One nearly hit a family member. Then when the power sander was on the floor one day, unplugged. It flew into the air."

Last spring, the DIEPART team investigated the Old Governor's Mansion in Des Moines. "It's a beautiful building," says Berger. "Five or six stories high with offices inside for lawyers, doctors. We were investigating for a woman who had a loft office there. She noticed things she couldn't explain."

When the team played back the video they had recorded in the basement and the first floor, they saw the orbs. Berger watched as one of them flew off another team member's head, then disappeared. "One of them flew over another one. Then one pursued the other."

Berger is most interested in the interactive ghosts, the ones that respond to the living. "We had EVP recordings where one of the team is training another and the voice on the recording says, 'Stupid teacher,'" says Berger. "EVPs come in underneath the 30 to 40 megahertz threshold. The sounds could be residual. If I applied a charge to a cassette tape, it'd record. Since a house is made out of wood carbon, it can hold a charge, too. Paranormal activity might be like a camera, recording the information. But that doesn't explain the interactive ghosts. We have to keep an open mind."

So You Want to Be a Paranormal Investigator

What does it take to be a paranormal investigator? The competition is stiff, although it's a volunteer position. There are only 60 members in the Iowa Paranormal Advanced Research Team (IPART), the umbrella organization that includes satellite organizations like DIEPART and SCIPART. Often only 10 or 15 members of the team go together to investigate a haunting or a UFO sighting.

"As a team, we are together for 12 or 15 hours straight," says Joe, the founder of DIEPART. "We sit in the dark together. So we have to get along. We don't want anyone who's difficult to be with. We don't want anyone who says right away that there's a ghost in the house. We want our team members to be skeptical."

The screening process begins with e-mail exchanges. Then Joe and the other team members talk with the applicant. "We try to weed out the crazies," says Joe. "When we question them, we try to discover whether their responses are consistent. We ask the same questions over and over again. We look for strange behavior, such as bipolar illness or schizophrenia." Team members are trained to question the potential clients and evaluate their responses.

Prospective investigators fill out a 50-question survey about their family and their schedules. Then they are given a profile and background check by state and federal agencies. If they pass those tests, they'll get an interview and be able to go on three investigations. If they pass that test, they'll have to attend boot camp and get the required certifications. Boot camp is an annual event that lasts from 8:00 a.m. to 8:00 p.m.

"By the time you get out of boot camp, you should be able to teach someone else how to work the equipment," says Joe. "It's intense."

The investigator can get some more certifications on his or her own. "You need common sense," says Joe. "You don't need a degree in parapsychology to be an investigator. You need to learn the basics from a group that's moderate. You could be the next pioneer in the field. There are no experts. People who claim to be experts aren't—unless they've died and happened to see the other side and come back to earth. No one really knows. A big chunk of it is unexplainable."

The training continues even after the team members are certified. Once a year, team members visit a site on the 10 most-haunted list.

This past year, they visited the Lemp Mansion in St. Louis, Missouri. The mansion, the site of many murders, was owned by Charles Lemp, who owned the Lemp Brewery.

When Prohibition hit, Lemp was bankrupted. Though his brewery and mansion were worth millions, he was forced to sell them for $500,000. He went back home and committed suicide in the basement. His wife, Lillian, found him hanging from the rafter. A short time afterward, she committed suicide, herself.

The mansion is now a bed and breakfast. The gift shop sells T-shirts with the slogan "Ghost to Ghost." Joe and his wife and their five-month-old son, Joe, stayed in the lilac room, Lillian's room. She was called the Lavender Lady of high society.

"Mrs. Lemp would only wear lilac-colored clothing," says Joe. "Her room was also painted that color."

The mansion is close to 7,500 square feet with 33 rooms. Mr. Lemp used an underground tunnel to travel between the brewery and his bedroom. Today, the basement houses memorabilia from the Lemp Brewery. The team set up their cameras and other equipment downstairs.

"We didn't pick up any evidence of a ghost there," says Joe. "But other people have. Having a paranormal experience is like being struck by lightning. It's not an everyday thing."

The investigator trainees learn how to screen clients, using another intensive questionnaire. "You never know until you set foot in a place whether the client is bona fide," says Joe. "Since I don't want my team to be in harm's way, we are very careful about screening applicants."

DIEPART team members have to know when a case has been faked. Recently, the team caught one set of clients making objects levitate on strings suspended from the ceiling. The wife wanted to break a lease on the apartment; when her husband disagreed, she pretended to see ghosts.

"Psychology is the most important part of investigating," says Joe. "Is there really paranormal activity happening? Sometimes people who are mentally ill claim they've seen ghosts. It could be that they're more attuned to the paranormal, or they could just be hallucinating."

When people's paranormal experiences aren't caused by fakery or mental illness, the DIEPART investigation validates their claims. "We're there to help them. When people invite us into their lives, we have to examine the psychological component. You look at the back of the picture and see the frame. We examine everything—the backing, the paper. We're more critical than the person they live with," says Joe.

Five to 20 investigators go on each case. The team stays up all night until early morning, collecting data. There are many jobs to perform, including setting up and monitoring the equipment.

A prerequisite for being on the DIEPART team is understanding how to use the equipment. "Other groups let people specialize. We don't," says Joe. "Everyone has to be up on the digital voice recorder and the soft laser thermometer. Everyone is responsible for it."

Team members do have different responsibilities, however. The leads on each floor are the bosses. They roam the floors and check what's going on. They investigate paranormal claims made by their colleagues. "If a team member claims to hear a noise, the lead tries to debunk it," says Joe. "The leader could find out that the rapping sound is coming from a radiator."

Throughout the night, the team rotates floors. The archivist documents everything, moving freely from floor to floor, keeping a chronology of events. He or she documents where someone has found a cold spot and checks to see that the equipment is working properly.

"Organizations that don't have an archivist often can't remember what happened on their latest case," says Joe. "We post our data right on our website. An investigation has to have a chronological synopsis."

The DIEPART team also learns about the history of a building. Understanding who the residents were in the past can help investigators guess the identity of the apparitions. "We interview the owner," says Joe. "Sometimes owners will have done research themselves to try to find out what's going on."

For people who become IPART team members, the paranormal can be a weekly event, since the group conducts one investigation per week. Their weekends become high tech slumber parties, gathering and interpreting data about real ghost stories. What better way to experience the paranormal firsthand?

Ghostly Places

Black Angel

OAKLAND CEMETERY, IOWA CITY, IOWA

On Halloween night in 1970, a young man named Larry visited the nine-foot-tall Black Angel statue that towers over the other headstones at Oakland Cemetery. The bronze statue, which looks down instead of up, has long wings. No one is certain why the statue stays so black. Some residents say that the statue was struck by lightning. Others say that the statue turned black because the lover of the deceased was unfaithful. The statue is said to possess certain powers to bring luck or take it away.

The monument was created by Teresa Dolezal Feldevert, a resident of Iowa City in the 1880s. She had been a doctor in Bohemia, but was unable to work in her profession in the United States. In 1891, her 18-year-old son by her first marriage, Eddie, died of meningitis. He was buried under a tree trunk in Oakland Cemetery.

Soon afterward, Teresa married Nicholas Feldevert and moved to Oregon. After Nicholas died in 1911, Teresa commissioned Mario Korbel to create the angel statue. She was unhappy with it because it didn't include a replica of the tree trunk marker, and she refused to pay his $5,000 fee. Korbel took her to court, and she was forced to pay him.

As she grew older, she often visited the statue, unhappy that it had turned black. She brought along rags to wipe the blackness off, without effect. After she died, her ashes were placed beside her husband and son.

The inscription says, in Hungarian:

For me the road was thorny
Without the comforts during the days of my life

So I would do anything for this world.
Hands clasped and head bowing my soul flies to eternity
Where after frustration you wait for the everlasting reward.

There is no date of death on her headstone.

On a dark and dreary Halloween night, 16-year-old Larry decided to destroy the angel. In those days, it was easy to sneak into the cemetery unnoticed. He and his friends walked softly on the leaves to the base of the statue. One of his friends looked at the Hungarian inscription and asked Larry what it meant.

Larry took out a sledgehammer from his backpack and jumped on the base of the statue. "It means 'Smash me!'" he cried. Just as Larry was going to strike the wing and break off a piece as a souvenir, the wind came up. He fell to the ground on his wrist. He got up, trying to hide how injured he was.

"Let's come back tomorrow night," he said. His friends agreed.

At home, Larry noticed that his wrist was bruised and he had no feeling in his hand. His mother took him to the doctor. The doctor told Larry's mother that her son would be fine. He didn't have any broken bones or ligaments. He just had a bad bruise.

Then Larry's arm got worse; the black bruise and numbness spread so that he couldn't use his arm at all. He stayed home from school, hoping to get better.

By the time Larry visited the Black Angel five days later, his arm was black up to his shoulder. He returned to the cemetery with his friends. The wind spun around them, blowing leaves in their faces.

"Let's go back, Larry. I don't want to go any farther."

"Come on, Paul. Nothing'll hurt you here," said Larry.

While his friends surrounded him, Larry touched the angel with his good hand and apologized. When he awakened the next morning, his bruise was gone. He never visited the Black Angel again.

TEAM DIEPART'S INVESTIGATION

On Wednesday October 12, 2005, team DIEPART investigated the statue. There had been reports of a glowing shape walking through the cemetery. Some people said it was the spirit of the Black Angel.

That night, the team captured some EVPs. They watched white light rise up from the statue. While they took photos, they felt as if they were being watched. In the process of doing their research, they did not touch the statue. They were careful not to harm it in any way.

Most of the stories about the Black Angel have to do with people who have touched the statue or desecrated it in some way. One young man urinated on the statue and died later in a car wreck. Another young man who used a hacksaw to cut off several fingers was later found floating in the Chicago River, after apparently having been strangled to death, a thumbprint on his throat. The coroner later found a thumb at the base of the Black Angel.

Everyone in Iowa City knows that you should never visit the Black Angel alone at night. If you want to see it during the day, stay back and look at it. Don't desecrate it, whatever you do. You'll probably regret it.

Cedar Rapids Library

CEDAR RAPIDS, IOWA

Elizabeth Schoenfelder, a retired librarian, told this story years ago to the local newspaper, the *Gazette*. Her story appeared on KCRG, a Cedar Rapids TV station, as part of their *Haunted Eastern Iowa* series

Every day, a woman named Helen Stein came into the Cedar Rapids Library to read the newspapers. She wore the same blue sweater every day. She usually stayed for about an hour and then left.

Helen came into the library for many years. Schoenfelder, who was used to seeing her, went on with her work, without giving Helen more than a glance.

One morning when Helen came in, Schoenfelder noticed that she was wearing some new clothes. "She looked all dressed up. I thought she must have come into some money. I'd never seen her look like that," said Schoenfelder.

Helen sat down and read the papers and then left. Schoenfelder was busy answering the phone, so she barely paid any attention to Helen. When it was about time for Schoenfelder to take her lunch break, Bill walked in. He approached the circulation desk and said, "Elizabeth, you've lost one of your most loyal patrons."

Schoenfelder looked up and asked, "Who?"

"Helen," replied Bill.

"But I just saw Helen a couple of hours ago."

"That couldn't be. She's dead."

"She was here at 10:30 a.m. She was about ten feet away from me."

Bill looked at Elizabeth, speechless for a moment. "Helen died at 3:30 in the morning. She suffocated when her house burned."

Elizabeth was quiet for a moment. She wondered who or what she had seen. To this day, Helen's spirit haunts the Cedar Rapids library.

Clear Lake Cornfield

CLEAR LAKE, IOWA

On February 3, 1959, 22-year-old Buddy Holly, 17-year-old Ritchie Valens, and 28-year-old J.P. "The Big Bopper" Richardson had just finished their gig at the Surf Ballroom in Clear Lake, Iowa. Buddy Holly and his band, The Crickets, had several number-one records on the Hit Parade, including "That'll Be the Day" and "Peggy Sue." Dion and the Belmonts, Frankie Sardo, and Waylon Jennings backed up the other musicians. They were on their way to the next leg of their "Winter Dance Party Tour," a concert in Fargo, North Dakota. A converted school bus that they had been traveling in had broken down, so with the help of the owner of the Surf Ballroom, Holly, Valens, and Richardson rented a light plane. Dion and the Belmonts stayed in the bus; they couldn't afford the $35 fare for the plane.

Their pilot, 21-year-old Roger Peterson, took off from Mason City with the three passengers at one a.m. As soon as they were aloft, they lost radio contact. A novice pilot, Peterson was not trained to fly by instruments and didn't know that they were heading straight into a blizzard. Peterson soon became disoriented by the snowstorm. The plane descended instead of ascending. It crashed into a cornfield five miles northeast of the airport, on the Albert Juhl farm.

A few hours later, after friends had tried to contact them, their bodies were found. They had been thrown away from the crash site. At nine a.m. the next morning, DJs around the nation informed their shocked audiences about "the night the music died."

Visitors to this Iowa cornfield have seen mysterious figures rising from the fields. Others say they hear music in the distance, music that could be played by Buddy Holly.

Coe College

CEDAR RAPIDS, IOWA

On October 12, 1918, a young Coe College student named Helen Esther Roberts died of the Spanish Flu in the women's dormitory. Her spirit has haunted the building ever since. Mention the name "Helen" to students, and they know who you're talking about. Recently, KCRG TV reported the haunting in their *Haunted Eastern Iowa* series.

"Things fly off the walls. Posters won't stay up," Erin Linning, an employee of Coe College, told KCRG. "Books slide off the shelves." People have also reported hearing strange noises late at night.

Student Jackie Briso said that the apparition appears most often on Halloween. The ghost, which appears like a white mist or glow, moves through room 219 of Voorhees Hall, where Helen died.

Confederate Ghost Soldiers

DAVENPORT, IOWA

Residents who live near the house on Brady Street in Davenport, Iowa, are often awakened in the middle of the night. Sometimes they hear dogs barking, cannons firing, and people moaning.

The owners of the house, the Youngs, asked Abigail de la Badie, an investigator from the International Ghost Hunters Society, to look into the matter. Family members saw an apparition in "gray misty form" walk through the rooms. Ashtrays and other small objects disappeared and often turned up in other places, like the basement. Doors slammed shut when no one was there.

The Youngs were not afraid of the ghost; in fact, Damon Young told Abigail they got a deal on the house because it was haunted. Though he felt as if he was being watched, he wasn't afraid. When he heard the gun shots, he called the police. Every time the police came, they couldn't find anything wrong. No one in the neighborhood had fired a gun.

Abigail began her investigation by studying the history of the house. The previous owners, the Cowherds, often couldn't sleep in the house. They were awakened by noises at night.

One of the former residents, Andrew Wyatt, was an avid Civil War reenactor as a member of the 4th Iowa Mounted Rifles. He would notice that the buttons on his uniforms had disappeared. His prized sword disap-peared and turned up in the basement. Downstairs, he heard someone singing "Dixie" and "Battle Cry of Freedom."

Abigail concluded that the house had some connection to the Civil War, so she contacted the Iowa State Historical Society. She discovered that there had been a prisoner of war camp for Confederate soldiers from December 1863 to July 1865 on Arsenal Island in the Mississippi River between Davenport and Rock Island, Illinois.

The conditions at the prison were harsh. Many of the soldiers had been captured after the Battle of Lookout Mountain in Tennessee, November 1863. The soldiers were not dressed for the harsh Iowa winter. By the end of the first month, over 5,600 Confederate soldiers were held there. Many died of disease and starvation.

Abigail learned that the 4th Iowa Mounted Rifles had been used to guard the prison. The guards were quick to shoot the prisoners. Many of the prisoners were afraid to sleep on the upper bunks because the Iowa soldiers would shoot them during the night. So they slept on the floor.

In her research, Abigail discovered that the Cowherd who had owned the house was descended from Private Peter Cowherd of C Company, 108th U.S. Colored Infantry, a man who used to be a slave. Peter was accused of shooting his former owner, John P. McClanahan of Company D, 9th Tennessee Infantry, who had paid Cowherd to let him escape.

Another prisoner, Private T. W. Grantham, tried to escape many times. He dug a tunnel to the outside. Once, he got beyond the fence and managed to get across the frozen river before he was captured and brought back to the prison.

Finally, he dressed up like a Union soldier and walked out the front gate. Chased by dogs and local police, he escaped to Davenport, though he was wounded in the thigh. He hid in the Youngs' house on Brady Street, where he died from the blood loss. His dying words were about his love for wife and two sons.

Does Private Grantham's ghost haunt the Youngs' house? Maybe the moans Damon heard were the soldier sobbing that he'd never see his wife and two sons again.

Cresco Theatre

CRESCO, IOWA

The Cresco Theatre, built in 1915, is an old place that was a popular stage for vaudeville acts in the 1920s and '30s. Formerly called the Cresco Opera House, it was renovated during the 1970s. The building was restored to its former grandeur with a jeweled chandelier in the entranceway and hand-painted murals on the walls. Today, the theatre has live performances, as well as movies shown on the stage. But when the theatre opened again, members of the audience noticed strange things happening.

Starting at the time of the renovation, guests and staff reported seeing paranormal activity there. Many people saw full-bodied apparitions in the theatre.

Investigators Chad Lewis and Terry Fisk have published the results of their research into the Cresco Theatre in their book, *The Iowa Road Guide to Haunted Locations*. Lewis said he had heard about the haunting of the old opera theatre from witnesses who reported seeing apparitions. He told the *Cresco Times* that staff had said that the ghost fooled around with lighting equipment. Other people have seen shadowy mysterious figures that look like old vaudeville stars, or reported hearing footsteps and noticing temperature changes when no one else was there.

Today when people come to the theatre, they know that the show isn't limited to the stage.

Currier Hall

UNIVERSITY OF IOWA, IOWA CITY
NAMES FICTIONALIZED

Todd Ristau included this site in his haunted tour of the University of Iowa. He also published a story about it on his website, *Third Eye Over Iowa*.

Currier Hall is filled with strange noises. Students who live there have heard low female voices surrounding them as they walk through the hall. They soon discover that no one is there.

Doors open and shut on their own. Cold drafts follow people as they enter the dormitory. Most of the ghostly happenings are on the fourth floor, where three students lived around 1912, when it was a dormitory for women.

According to the story told on campus, Sarah, Mary, and Angela shared a room and became close friends. They were rarely apart and could often be seen studying together at the library. One night in early spring, Sarah looked so happy that Angela asked her what had happened. Sarah shook her head and said it was a surprise. She'd tell Angela later that night.

But Sarah never did tell. Soon Angela was smiling herself. Mary asked her why she was so happy. Finally, Angela told Mary she had met a man. Mary giggled and said she had met someone, too. They wondered what secret Sarah was keeping from them.

During exams, they all found out. As the three of them walked toward the library, a handsome guy with dark hair and a mustache approached them.

Sarah brightened up and grabbed his arm, though he pretended not to know her. "Paul, I know a great place to go dancing Saturday night."

Then Angela said, "Henry, I got the flowers you sent me."

Mary looked him squarely in the eye. "Jim, we know your real identity."

The man shrugged his shoulders and ran. The three women looked at one another. When they returned to the dorm, they didn't feel any better. The mystery man had lied to them all and expected them not to say anything. One legend says that the three of them committed suicide by jumping out of the window; in other versions, they drank poison or shot themselves. However they met their deaths, they appear to have become permanent residents at Currier Hall.

Eldridge Bridge

ELDRIDGE, IOWA

Residents of Eldridge, in eastern Iowa, say the old two-lane bridge that crosses Lost Creek is haunted by the ghost of a schoolteacher. If you visit the bridge at night, according to the legend, you can see the apparition of the woman. She dresses in eighteenth-century clothes and wears a bonnet. If you stare at her too long, she'll disappear.

The legend says that the woman jumped from the bridge after having an argument with her husband. Her body wasn't discovered for several months. No wonder visitors often have a feeling of dread when they stand on the bridge and look down at the flowing waters of the creek.

If you dare visit on a moonlit night, you may see her walking up and down the bridge, wearing her blue gingham dress and white bonnet.

Fairview Cemetery

COUNCIL BLUFFS, IOWA

Council Bluffs is a hilly area cut by valleys. The Loess Hills, which border the Missouri River, are made up of fine quartz silt. The water erosion has made the hills look like small mountains. In the early 1800s, Lewis and Clark traveled through the Council Bluffs area, which became a gateway for western expansion. Naturally, this rugged area of western Iowa has many reported hauntings.

Hidden in the hills is the Fairview Cemetery, which has documented cases of apparitions. The oldest Mormon cemetery in Council Bluffs, with graves dating back to the 1840s, it's the burial place of General Grenville M. Dodge, whose house still stands in Council Bluffs at the top of a hill.

But his ghost has taken a back seat to another, the ghost of Carmelita, a young girl who died in 1930. She is said to haunt the cemetery.

Dark-haired Carmelita was only a year old when she died. Council Bluffs residents say that she doesn't know she's dead. She romps around the cemetery, chasing squirrels and robins. Visitors to the cemetery hear her giggle, and investigators have preserved her laughter on tape.

Often, she appears on top of her headstone, dressed in a white dress, her curls dangling over her shoulders. Don't be annoyed by her giggles. Stay and talk to her for as long as you can.

Grand Opera House

DUBUQUE, IOWA

The Grand Opera House was always rumored to be haunted, but the spirits there had been peaceful—until a renovation began several years ago. The workmen renovating the 1889 theatre stirred up many of the spirits during their restoration of the auditorium and other rooms.

Over the years, the theatre presented over 2,600 live performances that included stars like Henry Fonda, Ethel Barrymore, George M. Cohan, and Lillian Russell. One of the best-known productions was a lavish production of Ben Hur that featured horses, elephants, and chariots on the stage.

For a short time, the Grand Opera House became a movie theatre. But by 1986, the Opera House changed ownership once more and returned to being a theatre.

Throughout its history, guests have reported seeing ghosts there. One woman screamed during the first act of a play and ran out of the theatre. She told the police she had seen a ghost hovering over the orchestra pit. Other people claim the apparitions are long-dead actors.

Other theatre-goers reported hearing strange noises, including the moans of elephants and the clomp of horse hooves. Some hear the voice of Ethel Barrymore, who appeared on film during the 1920s. Often the cleaning ladies saw the ghosts sitting in the auditorium seats. When they approached them, the apparitions vanished.

You can visit the new Grand Old Opera today. It's open every day for performances. Be sure to bring your infrared camera in case you see a ghost appearing with the actors on stage.

Greenwood Cemetery

MATLOCK, IOWA

This cemetery, which is located on a gravel crossroads, is said to be the oldest one in Iowa. Its graves date from the early to mid-eighteenth century. Ghost hunters have visited this site many times. In fact, several of them recorded their findings on a seven-minute video that was posted on YouTube.

The ghost hunters visited the cemetery late at night and with their flashlights in hand, looked for lichen patterns on the gravestones. Their film, entitled *Greenwood Cemetery*, appears on YouTube. In the video, the ghost hunters talk about the details of their investigation. They discovered that several of the gravestones had lichen that took on an image of the person who was buried underneath.

After walking through the cemetery, they found that the trees on the crossroad formed a five-pointed star. Each tree was 13 steps away from the other tree. The ghost hunters couldn't explain why the trees formed a pentacle. Was it just a coincidence? Or was it a message from the creators of the cemetery?

Haunted First Street Bridge

DES MOINES, IOWA

David Ross, the owner of Natural History Tours, took his guests to this site. This is his story of the haunted First Street Bridge. This story also appeared in Ghosts of Polk County, Iowa, *by Tom Welch.*

At the turn of the twentieth century, an orphan boy named Sonny wandered through Des Moines begging for food. Desperate, he lived under the covered First Street Bridge at the confluence of the Raccoon and Des Moines rivers.

An old lady took pity on him and brought him into her house. She wanted to give him an education, but he didn't want any of that. One night, he took a sheet, wound it on the bed, and climbed out the window.

Des Moines residents soon saw him begging on the street again. He again slept beneath First Street Bridge and drank from the Raccoon River that flowed underneath it. He wore tattered clothes and became thinner and thinner. A lawyer who saw him on the bridge threw money at him.

One night when the lawyer crossed the bridge again, he saw Sonny. He pitied the poor boy. When the lawyer held out the money toward him, the child disappeared into thin air. What the lawyer did not know was that Sonny had drowned in the Raccoon River a few days earlier; children found his body washed up on the shore.

The sightings of Sonny continue to this day. Fishermen on Scott Street look west to First Street and see Sonny's ghost appear and disappear.

Historic Dodge House

COUNCIL BLUFFS, IOWA

This three-story Victorian mansion was built in 1869 by one of the most influential Iowans. General Grenville M. Dodge was a Civil War veteran who was closely connected to Presidents Abraham Lincoln and Ulysses S. Grant. In 1866, Dodge became a U.S. Congressman, as well as Chief Engineer of the Union Pacific Railroad.

His house sits on a terrace that overlooks the Missouri River Valley. Now preserved as a historic site, it has retained the luxurious amenities of that day, like parquet floors and cherry and butternut woodwork chosen by his wife Ruth Anne. The mirrors even have embedded diamond dust in them. Dodge's office remains as it was when he lived there, his Winchester rifle resting on the mantel.

Many people who take the tour of the house today are unaware that it is haunted. Every year close to Halloween, storytellers begin their haunted tour of Council Bluffs, visiting the Squirrel Cage Jail and other haunted sites. The Historic Dodge House is a staple of the tour.

Jeffrey Raia, a member of PRISM (Paranormal Research and Investigative Studies Midwest), captured a photo of an apparition at the Dodge House in 2004. The photo showed a ghostly young girl looking through the window of the front door. Is the Dodge House haunted by her? Is that apparition Dodge's daughter? We may never know for sure.

Historic Wickham House

COUNCIL BLUFFS, IOWA

The Wickham House is a Victorian mansion built in the nineteenth century that's often included in the ghostly tours of Council Bluffs. The house, now a bed-and-breakfast, is listed on the National Register of Historic Places. The Wickham brothers were the architects who designed the Squirrel Cage Jail.

People who stay in the mansion have reported seeing an apparition in the parlor. The woman is dressed in nineteenth-century clothing. Mrs. Wickham's mahogany casket had been laid out in the parlor after she passed on. Could they be seeing her ghost?

Iowa State University
Haunted Tour

AMES, IOWA

Every year at Halloween, Iowa State University hosts a tour of haunted sites on campus. At 6:00 p.m., people meet with their flashlights in hand, prepared to weather the rainy night and the ghostly figures. The walking tour includes stops at Campanile, Memorial Union, Bearshar and Catt and Mackey Halls, C. Y. Stephens Auditorium, the Farm House Museum, and the ISU cemetery. The group takes short jaunts into the buildings, looking for hauntings. Many of the ISU ghost stories have been published in local newspapers over the college's 150-year history.

No wonder over 370 people showed up for the event in 2007. The group was so large that people divided up into small groups, ready to meet the ghosts that inhabit the buildings.

First, the tour visits the underground corridor where the ghost of C. Y. Stephens appears. On the Halloween walk, people have seen apparitions in the corridor between the auditorium and the coliseum that look like Stephens. As they walk, they often feel cold drafts and a wind that sears their cheeks.

The auditorium can't hold a candle to the Memorial Union, which pays homage to fallen ISU graduates. Visitors have heard moans when they stand inside the building. No one can explain why it happens. But the name Hortense Wind often comes up, the only female name listed among the fallen war heroes in Gold Star Hall.

According to Neva Peterson, a ghost opens the curtains of the second-floor bedroom at the Farm House Museum. Visitors there have also heard the dressers rattle and tapping sounds, as well as seeing lights being turned on and off.

The ghost of Frederica Shattuck, the founder of the Iowa State Players, appears all over campus. Shattuck came to ISU in 1914 as the first director of the theatre. She pushed hard to establish the theatre at ISU, since many people weren't interested. The theatre building was named in her honor in 1960. She died in 1969. Though she first haunted Shattuck Theatre, when the building was torn down in 1979 and the players moved to Fisher Theatre, the ghost of Shattuck followed. In a 1978 *Iowa State Daily* article, speech professor Sherry Hoopes told the story of Shattuck's wheelchair. The cast members heard strange noises and saw that Shattuck's wheelchair, which she had donated to the program, had rolled across the stage. The empty wheelchair stopped, facing the audience, as if the ghost were about ready to deliver a speech. Another actor heard his name screamed out when no one was there. Burt Drexler, a former ISU speech professor, told the *Iowa State Daily* that the lights in the auditorium have been observed to go on and off by themselves.

Assistant Professor Joseph Kowalski, who was looking for the backstage lights, heard a voice tell him, "The lights are by the door." Another time, when Kowalski was working in the costume shop, objects like scissors and a tape measure disappeared. In 1993, he told Ken Uy, a reporter for the *Ames Daily Tribune*, that those objects disappeared and reappeared in other places. Kowalski reported that he was one of three witnesses who heard music come on over the loudspeakers spontaneously. Brooks Chelsvig, the sound technician, and Joe Libby, the former house manager, went upstairs to see what was going on. They found no one there.

One of the theatre students quoted in the article was Molly Harrington, who told the reporter, "She's just letting us know she's still around. She's telling us she's glad we're doing theatre at ISU, since she was the one who started it."

Even if you don't see the Shattuck ghost, you can still have fun on the Halloween walk. Ms. Sheridan, who leads the tour, says everyone enjoys doing the walking tour each year. And after you're finished, you can stop at the haunted Farm House Museum for hot chocolate and Halloween treats.

Jordan House

WEST DES MOINES, IOWA

The Jordan House is one of the most popular sites in Des Moines. People from all over the world visit the house, which is haunted by James Cunningham Jordan's daughter, Edy.

James came from Virginia to build his log cabin in Valley Junction, now West Des Moines, in 1849. Built in stages, the house grew into a 16-room Italian Gothic mansion. He lived there with his wife, Melinda, and their six children. Listed on the National Register, Jordan House, now a museum, is the oldest building in Polk County and West Des Moines.

Jordan, a prominent member of the community, helped bring the railroad to Des Moines to transport his cattle to market. While he built his business and became wealthier, Jordan became a staunch abolitionist in a state where pro-slavers were in the majority. His home was a hiding place for slaves and other fugitives, such as John Brown, the notorious raider of Harpers Ferry. Brown was a guest in Jordan's home many times. *Iowa: Its History and Its Foremost Citizens*, published in 1915, says that Brown "more than once received assistance in different ways from Mr. Jordan." Jordan was referred to as the "chief conductor" of the Underground Railroad.

Edy, who died as a young child, loved to play practical jokes. She would never listen to her parents. She often slid down the banister squealing, then jumped down onto the floor. Watching her fall one time, her father told her to stay away from the banister. But Edy just giggled. She never obeyed him.

One day, Edy slid down the banister and fell. Her mother heard the crashing sound and ran into the front hall. Edy was on the floor. She carried Edy's limp body to the bedroom. She sent for a doctor, who told her that Edy had broken her neck. There was little he could do for her. By the time Jordan got home, Edy was barely breathing. His wife was sobbing and Jordan held her tightly.

The Jordan family kept a vigil at her bedside for three days, until Edy died. She never spoke again. Jordan began talking about Edy as a ghost to keep her memory alive.

Today, visitors to the Jordan House often see Edy on the stairs with her cat. She waves and then disappears. Perhaps her father did keep her spirit alive.

KD Station

SIOUX CITY, IOWA

KD Station, a meat-packing plant built in 1918, was so haunted the owner advertised the fact.

The austere building has a sad history. After it was built, the company went bankrupt. The Swift Company purchased it in 1919 and packed its meat there until December 14, 1949, when a gas leak caused an explosion, killing 21 employees and injuring 91. Many of these employees are said to haunt the building.

In 1976, another company, owned by Kermit Lohry, renovated the building. Two years later, it reopened as a shopping center with a bowling alley and a golf course. A man who worked security in the building reported that he saw strange things there. One night, he turned off the lights on the terrace, only to discover they were back on again. He noticed that the elevators' knobs were moving when the elevators were standing still. For years, the brochure for the shopping center said, "Paul Pulaski, our in-house ghost, welcomes you!"

Now that brochure is a piece of history. Two fires changed the fate of the building forever. In 2006, a fire broke out in the fourth-floor bowling alley. The fire department proved that it was arson. The building couldn't recover. Today, it's abandoned, leaving the burnt-out entrails to the remaining spirits who dare to occupy it.

Kate Shelley Bridge

BOONE, IOWA

One day in 1881, torrential rains caused Honey Creek to flood and the bridge spanning it to collapse. The water from the creek overflowed onto the Shelleys' farm. Kate was just 15 then. She had lost her father, who, in addition to running their farm, had worked for the Chicago and Northwestern Railroad. Her mother, now a widow, was running the farm herself.

The tracks of the railroad passed behind their fields. Kate knew that the express train was on the way. It would travel over the Des Moines River bridge at midnight, and then it would head to the washed-out Honey Creek Bridge. Kate knew she had to do everything she could to avert disaster.

Taking her father's lantern, she headed out to the Moingona station, where the train would make its last stop before traveling to the Des Moines River bridge. She walked through the flooded land with only the light of a lantern. She climbed up the hills toward the bridge, struggling to keep her footing on the wet earth. Below her, there was only the raging river and a 50-foot descent. The water was rushing up toward her. The bridge was so high that the railroad never let anyone walk on the tracks. The wind was so strong it nearly blew her over. Her lantern light went out for a moment. She shook it and it came back on. She stretched her arms out so she'd be able to maintain her balance as she walked.

By the time she reached the Moingona station, only a mile away, she was exhausted. She shouted, "The Honey Creek Bridge is down!" as she walked, hoping people would hear her. At the station, the stationmaster telegraphed her message to Ogden. The train stopped there, saving the passengers' lives.

Then she found out that that the pusher engine had gone ahead with four people aboard. So Kate got on another pusher engine that set out to rescue them. By the time they found them, two of the four were clinging to a tree in the water that was caught by the bridge. The other two had drowned.

The following day, everyone knew Kate's name. She was a heroine. The townspeople raised money to help her family. Kate was awarded with a scholarship to Simpson College in Indianola. She graduated as a teacher and taught in Boone for many years. In 1903, she took a position in Moingona County as a station agent. Kate died in 1912 of Bright's disease, a few years after her mother died. She's buried in Sacred Heart Cemetery in Boone.

Boone residents say that her ghost still haunts the bridge. Many people have seen the young girl carrying a lantern, her arm reaching out in the darkness.

Martin Chapel Cemetery

MILLS COUNTY, IOWA

Martin Chapel Cemetery has over 500 unmarked graves and lots of ghosts. The cemetery, created by the Mormons in the mid-1800s, is behind the cliffs of Loess Hills in Mills County. The cemetery is dark at night, lit only by Interstate 29. If you want to visit it, make sure you don't go alone.

Carl Norgard, director of the Paranormal Research and Investigative Studies Midwest (PRISM), has made many visits to the cemetery. He told reporter Courtney Brummer of *The Daily Nonpareil* of Council Bluffs that this cemetery is a place for restless spirits. The grave diggers stick long metal rods into the ground before they begin opening a new plot. The rods tell them whether they will hit one of the unmarked graves.

On foggy nights, residents stay far away from the cemetery. Shadows are said to rise from the graves and stalk anyone who comes near them.

If you see a shadow, run the other way. Wait until daylight to visit the cemetery. That's when the restless spirits sleep.

Mary's Grave

HOMESTEAD, IOWA

During the nineteenth century, a six-year-old girl was traveling with her family through Iowa to California. Her father had heard that he could become rich panning for gold in the Sierra Nevada Mountains. When their covered wagon got close to Iowa City, the little girl, whose name was Mary Wright, got sick with a serious infection. She suffered for several days before she died August 19, 1854.

Her parents buried her in the Sprague Cemetery (now on Highway 6), just west of Homestead, which had been established shortly before the Civil War. When the railroad came through the town, many of the graves were moved. But not Mary's. It is still there to this day. In fact, visitors say that they can find her grave underneath a blue light that hovers over it on the last day of every year.

In 2007, reporter Josh Hinkle, from KCRG TV in Cedar Rapids, covered the haunting in the station's series *Haunted Eastern Iowa*. He interviewed Lori Erickson, who had included Mary's story in her book, *Ghosts of the Amana Colonies*. Lori talked about the people who had seen the blue aura over Mary's grave.

Then, on Halloween night in 2007, the DIEPART team came to investigate the gravesite, using a parabolic microphone. Joe and the team recorded EVPs that showed that "one spirit had been left behind." Maybe it was Mary's.

The Mason House Inn and Caboose Cottage

BENTONSPORT, IOWA

If you want to meet a ghost, be sure to stay at the Mason House Inn in Bentonsport, Iowa. You might meet one, or all five, of the spirits that inhabit the 160-year-old inn, which was used as a hospital during the Civil War and after the First World War. Three of the owners died in the inn, and someone was murdered in one of the rooms.

Owner Joy Hanson told About.com that several of her guests have had paranormal experiences. One of the guests saw the foggy image of a mischievous boy who plays tricks. Another guest saw an old lady in a nightgown and another one saw an elderly man. One guest, a minister, who was staying in Room 5, reported that something tugged on his sleeve while he was sleeping. Though he did not believe in ghosts before he came to the Mason House Inn, he changed his mind after seeing one.

Joy got more confirmations from a psychic who visited the inn. As she was checking in, she told Joy that that she could sense the spirits and that they were happy living in the inn. "They won't hurt anyone," she said. She described each one of the ghosts. She saw a boy (George) dressed in knickers, who is about 12 or 13 years old. He stays on the second landing. The old woman on the fifth floor enjoys looking through boxes. She wears a white nightgown and often vanishes and reappears.

In spite of the nice spirits, some guests get a bad feeling about Room 7, where a guest was killed—stabbed in the heart by another guest who mistook him for a robber. Guests often hear footsteps when no one is around.

Mary Frances "Fannie" Mason Kurtz, the last Mason to own the building, died in front of the fireplace in 1951. While eating lunch in the restaurant, one of the psychics saw Fannie walking around the room greeting visitors. Bill McDermet, a retired Congregationalist minister who bought the inn in 1989, claimed that he saw the ghost of Mary Mason Kurtz on the third floor, where he had an office. Kurtz told him that she was not happy with the renovations they were doing on the inn.

In fact, the ghosts went so far as to make design suggestions! After workmen removed the wallpaper, Bill and his wife would find the wallpaper on the walls again. One morning, they found the wallpaper sample book on the floor open to a page. They bought that design and put it up. That wallpaper stayed on the walls.

There is no shortage of candidates for who could be haunting the inn. Lewis Mason, a furniture maker who bought the hotel in 1857, also died there of cholera in 1867. His daughter died in the south bedroom on the third floor in 1911, when she was 83. His granddaughter, Fannie Mason Kurtz, died there at the age of 84 in 1951. She was sitting in the rocking chair for three days before anyone found her. Guests report hearing the sounds of the rocking chair, though it no longer exists.

Have Joy and her husband, Chuck, seen the ghosts? Joy told About.com that she has seen a tall, gaunt old man with white hair—"just a head, his body is a column of fog"—whom she's named "Mr. Foggybody." When she looks in the mirror on the second or third floor, she sees him behind her. She looks in the mirror again, and he's gone. She's seen him five times since June of 2001, when they moved in, after Chuck retired from the Air Force. She thinks he was Francis O. Clarkson, who was Lewis Mason's son-in-law. Though he didn't die in the inn, his body lay in the parlor for days during the wake. He's buried in the Bentonsport Cemetery. Joy's daughter has seen a floating head in Room 6, one that resembled Mr. Foggybody.

When Joy was dusting the floor upstairs, she heard footsteps that sounded like clomping boots. She called her husband's name, but no one was there. Instead she found him talking on the phone on the first floor. He told her he had been talking on the phone while she was upstairs.

Joy has found windows open when they had been shut and the front door locked when it had been left unlocked for guests. She found plastic bags beside the door and wondered if the ghost likes plastic Walmart bags.

Joy tells guests who stay at the Mason House Inn that they should expect visitors. They shouldn't be surprised if someone tugs on their clothes while they're asleep, or if they find a door ajar when they've closed it, or a window open. That's what it's like living with ghosts.

Mathias Ham House

DUBUQUE, IOWA

The Italianate-style house sits on a windy cliff overlooking the Mississippi River at the Iowa-Illinois-Wisconsin border. Mathias Ham, a shipping magnate, originally built a small stone house on the site in 1837. He later added a tower so he could watch the boats on the Mississippi River. In addition to shipping, Ham made money from mining lead, as well as cutting down trees for lumber.

The mansion had 14-foot ceilings and ornate furnishings. After his first wife, Margaret, died in 1856, he added more additions to the house, making it into a mansion with 24 rooms. He had two more children with his second wife, Zerelda. The mansion, which grew with his family, became the pride of Dubuque. A small staircase led up to the cupola on the top floor, where he used to watch his ships sail into the cove. He would often tell the police when pirates were boarding ships on the river. Many pirates were arrested. They vowed to take their revenge on him.

By the 1890s, everyone in the Ham family had died, except his daughter Sarah, who lived there alone for many years. One night when she was reading a book in her third-floor bedroom she heard a noise. She put her book down on the table, where she kept a gun in the drawer, and tiptoed downstairs, hoping she'd find out who was there.

She found no one. Scared, she told her neighbors what had happened. She told them she'd put a light in the window to let them know if the burglar had returned. The next night, she heard the sound again, as though someone was walking around on the first floor.

She walked outside her bedroom and cried, "Who's there?" There was only silence. She locked her door, put her light in the window, and took her gun out of the drawer and cocked it. She listened to the sound of footsteps walking across the front hall and held her breath as the clunking sound made its way up the steps to the third floor. Sarah shot her gun twice, hoping that her neighbors would be there soon to help her.

Her neighbors broke down the door and ran into the house. They followed a trail of blood out of the house to the Mississippi River banks, where they found the body of a pirate captain. Sarah had killed the intruder.

Did the pirate captain intend to kill Sarah? Was he there to take revenge on the Ham family? No one knows for sure.

Members of the Dubuque County Historical Society, which has owned the mansion since 1912, have reported icy cold spots on the third floor. They feel uncomfortable there. Some people say that the pirate captain haunts the stairway and the third floor, where he was shot.

There are odd, unexplained noises as well. Allegedly, a man hung himself in the cupola in the early 1900s. One night when the curator was unscrewing a light bulb, he heard a loud noise, the sound of a pipe organ. The Ham organ hasn't worked in decades. He screwed the bulb back in. The sound stopped.

One tour guide, named Jim, spent a night in the mansion in 1978. He reported feeling a strong presence in the house. By about three a.m., several entities made themselves visible to him. He wasn't scared easily.

He heard women's voices early in the morning. When he went to investigate the sounds, no one was there. He also heard footsteps on the second floor of the mansion and soft shuffling sounds in the basement. It was as though someone was leaving through a tunnel. (A tunnel just beyond the basement wall had collapsed many years previously.) He found a spring-locked window open in the morning.

In spite of the rumors of the Mathias Ham House being haunted, Tacie Campbell of the Dubuque County Historical Society, who's worked at the house for over 37 years, insists the story is apocryphal.

Says Campbell, "There never have been any pirates close to here. One couldn't have died near the house. This story just scares the children who come to visit. Some are so scared they won't come inside. I'm telling them that there's nothing to be afraid of."

Why not visit the Mathias Ham House and decide for yourself?

The Monroe Mansion

This huge three-story house, which was built in 1860, sits on the top of a cliff. The white house with blue shutters was built by Joseph Gwinn Long, a prominent businessman of Pennsylvania Dutch descent. He lived there with his wife, Regina, and their children. Long was active in the Monroe community, bringing in banks and financing real estate development. The mansion was his showpiece.

Regina was a stern woman who had two sons. One died when he was just a toddler. Then a girl was born. When she was five years old, the Long family moved into town to give their daughter more opportunities.

Over the years, many people have seen apparitions at the old mansion. Mists often rise from the floor to the ceiling. Though Mrs. Hart, the previous owner, had never seen a ghost, her husband and her father have seen the full-bodied apparition of a man. Word about the haunting spread through the town. Neighbors stay away from the old house once it gets dark.

"We didn't know it was haunted before we bought it," says Judy Salier, former owner of the mansion. She and her husband bought the house in 1990. "My husband, Mike, was in love with Victorian houses. He was also interested in the paranormal. When the renovations began, paint brushes would go missing and turn up in the master bedroom. The workmen got freaked out and wouldn't come back."

Mike, who was a corrections office supervisor at a prison, knew that the house was haunted. But it didn't bother him.

"This was my husband's dream home," says Judy. "He wanted to restore it. He was a burly man, who loved history and living in a small town. Every time he mentioned ghosts, I thought he was joking. He was a prankster."

"The house needed lots of work. We had painters coming in and out of it daily, doing cosmetic stuff, plastering in between the walls, framing the windows. Items would just disappear on their own."

The plumbers told Judy about the strange things that happened while they were working. One saw a female ghost fly in through the window and sit on the armchair. The apparition disappeared as he approached it.

As the renovations continued, the workmen reported their tools missing. "They accused one another of taking each other's tools," says Judy. "Still, the paint brushes, wrenches ended up in the master bedroom."

One Halloween, Judy and Mike had guests who witnessed bizarre events. "It was our favorite time there," says Judy. "One girlfriend of mine saw a punch bowl ladle levitate into the air. No one was holding it. It just stood there in the air. She flipped out. Then the door that was bolted popped open on the hutch. No one was there to do it.

"I've read ghost stories," says Judy. "But I wasn't a believer. Mike was seeing more than I did at that time. I thought he was exaggerating."

Unable to cope, the Saliers invited several paranormal teams to investigate. One paranormal team that came to the house heard dishes crashing and doors slamming and a sound like a chain moving across the second floor while they were on the first floor. One investigator ran upstairs and discovered that the room was empty. Then they heard a loud boom that came out of nowhere.

The one story that convinced Judy about the existence of ghosts was one that Paul, one of the workmen, told her. A recovering alcoholic, Paul helped Mike rebuild cars and trucks. One hot day, he and Mike were working on the transmission of an old Toyota. Paul felt overheated, so he went inside the house to get a cool drink of water. He walked through the dining room through the pocket doors on the north side of the library. He felt a coldness in the air. Then he saw a woman hanging in midair with no feet.

"Paul went ballistic and couldn't talk right," says Judy. "He described her to a relative of the people who had built the house, and they said it was Regina. In fact, on the first day we moved in the previous owners brought us a picture of Regina. Paul identified the ghost as Regina. She was wearing a white furry bonnet and white dress."

Other people saw full-bodied apparitions in the house. Judy's parents saw an apparition when they stayed in the upstairs bedroom on their way to Hawaii to visit Judy's brother. Judy's dad left the room one morning, and came back and saw a woman in white sitting at the north window. He left the room again. When he saw his wife, he asked her about sitting in the window in her white robe. She looked surprised and said, "I don't have a white robe."

Just after Judy's parents left, an accident occurred while Mike was working on an old Toyota Cruiser truck. He was alone at the mansion. Mike had the vehicle's axles propped up with cement blocks while he took the shock absorbers off. Something went wrong, and the car fell on Mike, crushing his chest and killing him.

Mike's death in 1997 was only the latest incident in the horrible history of the mansion. Tragedy came to anyone who lived there. One of the Long brothers committed suicide in the stairwell. The house was also used as an Underground Railroad stop, with tunnels that stretched south from under the barn to the hill. Slaves were hidden because Iowa had a bounty on blacks who entered the state.

Broken headstones mark the graves on the property. A local historian speculated that family members had died during the cholera epidemic.

"People ask why I still stay here, after Mike died in 1997," says Judy. "The place calms me and gives me solace. It grew on me. Financially, I'd be better off moving."

Judy has seen one apparition that actually comforts her. She has it on tape, and she and her children have watched it over and over again. Mike's face appears in the curtains in his room.

"It's there. It'd be just like Mike to do it. He was a prankster."

Mount Pleasant Cemetery

WASHTA, IOWA

This story has been told many times by the residents of Washta. Troy Taylor included it in his book, *Beyond the Grave*. Today it has become legendary. In the 1930s, an elderly couple named Olga and Heinrich Schultz owned a small farm there. Since they were older, they needed help with the chores. So one day, they hired a man named Will Florence. They gave him room and board as well as a small salary.

No matter how many questions Olga asked Will about his background, he never gave her the same story. First he told her he was recovering from a serious illness. Another time, he said he worked as a forest ranger. Olga didn't believe he'd ever done farm work before. That's what she told her husband.

While Will stayed with them, the economy got bad throughout the country. It was the Depression, and banks were closing. Washta was like other towns. One morning, Heinrich went to the bank to take out his money, but the building was closed. Other residents who were waiting in line recognized him. He was never seen alive again.

Several days later, the bodies of Heinrich and Olga were found at their farm house. Both had been struck on the head with an axe. Everything in their house was gone.

The sheriff started a search for Will Florence, who had disappeared. They captured him a few days later, in Nebraska. But they had no evidence to hold him, so he was released.

Then strange things started happening in Mount Pleasant Cemetery, where the Schultzes were buried. On the headstone, a face started to appear. The sheriff went there and looked at it himself. He recognized Florence.

The sheriff, who was superstitious, decided that the Schultzes were telling him who their murderer was—Will Florence. He looked at the evidence carefully once more and discovered he had overlooked a clue. He put out an arrest warrant for Florence. But he was unable to find him again. It was as if the man had disappeared off the face of the earth.

Old Indian Dam

AMANA COLONIES

In 1854, the Amana Colonies were established by the Inspirationalists from Buffalo, New York. The men and women who built these colonies were Germans who were unhappy with the Lutheran Church. They established their first "Community of True Inspiration" in Buffalo, where they lived a communal life.

When their first community became too populated and the city began to attract their young people, the leaders decided to move once again. They finally came to Iowa and settled beside the Iowa River valley. They called their community "Amana," which means "to remain faithful." The Amana communities were entirely self-sufficient, growing their own crops and having their own businesses to provide for every need. Religion and a simple lifestyle were central to their existence.

The Amana communities owned the area called the Indian Dam, located on the Iowa River. The area is wooded, with spots of rock outcroppings. Originally, the Sauk Indians lived there for thousands of years. They hunted game like buffalo, fished in the river for bass, and ate wild plants that grew there.

The Indian Dam, which was listed on the National Register of Historic Places, was built by the tribes over three hundred years ago. The stones of the dam shape a V that trapped crappie, largemouth bass, walleye, catfish, and white bass. Today, it's still known as a great area to fish.

An old fishing pier created by the Indians still remains there today. It can only be seen at low tide. To this day, boats can't travel around the pier or dam easily. They become marooned there, caught in the grass and mud.

Legends about the dam have grown over the years. The people of the Amana Colonies know that the areas where the Indians lived for thousands of years have a spooky feeling about them. On nights when the moon is full, near the dam, Amana residents hear the Indians beating their drums.

Rose Hill Cemetery

MISSOURI VALLEY, IOWA

Back in the late 1800s, the Chicago and Northwestern Railroad created this cemetery to bury the hobos who stole rides on the trains. The hobos often would ride on the roofs of the cars or hide inside the boxcars behind a crate. The engineers would do anything to get rid of these invaders, right up to clubbing them or throwing them underneath the train. There were plenty of other ways hobos could meet their ends as well, including starvation, exposure, accidents, and the occasional murder.

Later, their bodies were buried in unmarked graves in the back of Rose Hill Cemetery. Many bodies were piled on each other. People who have seen spectral apparitions there think that the hobos' spirits can't rest because of the way they were treated. Rita Miller, Missouri Valley City Clerk, told reporter Courtney Brummer of *The Daily Nonpareil* that she and her husband saw apparitions. What she and her husband witnessed was truly scary.

A mist comes up from the graveyard every night. Some of it swirls into shapes that look like shadow men. They seem to be unshaven hobos in tattered clothes. They moan and cry about how they were murdered.

Once the hobo apparitions, rising up from the hill top, chased Rita and her husband out of the cemetery. They vowed never to return there.

Visitors don't always heed Rita's warnings about the ghosts. Many have reported being tapped on the shoulder and hearing voices. Most don't stay in Rose Hill Cemetery very long.

Simpson College

INDIANOLA, IOWA

Simpson College, a liberal arts college located south of Des Moines, has a well-known haunting.

In the early twentieth-century, 21-year-old Mildred Hedges was a student there. Mildred's family had saved and sacrificed to give her a college education. She was a good, conscientious student, always doing more than her share.

One day, she was standing in the mezzanine in College Hall, which was a chapel during those days, holding a stack of papers in her arms. Somehow, she lost her balance and fell down the stairwell, breaking her neck. Mildred was taken to the college infirmary, where she later died.

Many students have seen the young woman carrying a stack of papers in her arms. Sometimes they see a light at the window or hear the sound of shuffling feet.

"We've had ghost hunters here investigating these phenomena," says Cynthia Dyers, librarian and archivist of Simpson College. "They've checked for vibrations and apparitions."

Though the apparitions have been less frequent recently, every year around Halloween, Mildred makes an appearance.

Sioux City Airport

Passengers on flights have seen strange occurrences at the Sioux City Airport. On July 19, 1989, United Flight 232 crashed there; 112 of the 372 passengers on board died.

The plane landed in a curtain of fire, skidding on the runway. The film of the crash was shown over and over again on the TV stations. It didn't appear as if that plane would make it. But, miraculously, it did.

The heroics of the crew on that flight are well known. The flight engineer jimmied the hydraulics to make the landing gear function, then used his own body weight to hold them down. If he hadn't been so heroic, the pilot couldn't have steered the injured plane to a full stop, and more people would have died.

Sioux City Airport is very small, with only two runways. It's outside of the small city, not used a lot like other airports. Not very many accidents have happened there. But on foggy nights, residents say that disembodied sounds appear out of nowhere. The sounds seem to shake the ground.

People have heard screams and moans. Sometimes passengers who look out the window of a plane see orbs floating on the tarmac. Maybe the ghosts of the passengers on Flight 232 have come back to visit.

Squirrel Cage Prison

COUNCIL BLUFFS, IOWA

The three-story-high Squirrel Cage Jail in Council Bluffs was the largest rotary jail ever built. William Brown and Benjamin Haugh of Indianapolis patented their idea for pie-shaped jail cells in 1881. This cell design gave maximum security by allowing the guards to stay away from the prisoners. Squirrel Cage Jail was in use from September 1885 to December 1969, and was notorious for the number of prisoners who died there. As a result, the prison became the most haunted site in Council Bluffs.

How did the prison become so deadly? The cells were arranged around a central tower, "many cages, so many theatres in which each actor is alone, perfectly individualized and constantly visible," according to one Iowa State professor, who called it "a device in which human welfare had been sacrificed for security and the convenience of the jailer."

In 1887, the *Council Bluffs Globe* called the Victorian Gothic–style jail, which then held 32 prisoners, a failure because the cages wouldn't rotate on the axis. The jail was reported to be in "filthy" condition and needed to be renovated and cleaned. By 1929, the Squirrel Cage had far exceeded its maximum capacity, housing over 165 prisoners.

The jail held notorious criminals like the "Mad Dog Killers," Charles Brown and Charles Kelley. The pair had killed a man while robbing a store in Omaha, Nebraska, in February 1961. The next day, in Council Bluffs, they shot Alvin Koerhsen five times and stole his car. When the car wouldn't start, they forced Kenneth Vencel to drive them before they threw him out of his car and shot him. Vencel survived and helped the police find the two criminals. Brown was executed on July 24, 1962—the first man to be executed in Iowa in more than a decade. Kelley was hanged September 6 of that year—the last person executed by the state of Iowa.

The cylinder of the jail is 28 feet high and 24 feet in diameter and weighs over 20,000 pounds empty. It's suspended from an iron beam on the fourth floor. The cylinder has three floors, each with ten pie-shaped cells that held two prisoners each. Each one was turned with a hand crank until the cell lined up with the floor, since there was only one entrance and exit. While the superintendent slept, a water wheel rotated the cell to give the prison added security. But the noise of the rotating cells kept the prisoners and the guards awake all night.

Many prisoners tried to break out, but only three succeeded. One was recaptured immediately when his father turned him in. The other two escaped to Missouri, only to be apprehended later.

Two prisoners died in their cells. One died of a heart attack. The other died climbing up to the ceiling to write his name. But these are not the ghosts that haunt the Squirrel Cage Jail.

The superintendent, J.M. Cater, who stayed at the prison the longest, is said to haunt it. Tourists, as well as staff members, have heard strange noises, rappings, and doors opening and shutting.

The jail looks the same today as it did when it was built. Visitors can sense the despair and anger that envelops the place, though no one lives there anymore.

Thirteen Stairs Cemetery

PLEASANT RIDGE, IOWA

The graves in the Thirteen Stairs Cemetery are very old, dating back to the 1800s. Visitors to the cemetery have seen apparitions and have been touched on the shoulder while walking through it. The stories about the haunted cemetery were so well known that a team of researchers from the Iowa Center for Paranormal Research came to investigate on several occasions.

In September of 2000, the team focused on the grave of Lucy, a young girl who had died over two hundred years ago. They found that they received high readings from their EMF detector near her headstone. They also photographed orbs sailing around Lucy's grave site. By the time they got to the back of the cemetery, they began feeling cold. The temperature readings had dropped considerably.

Feeling chilly and lightheaded, they continued to gather data that night. By the time they left, it was close to dawn. As they looked back, they saw a mist rise from Lucy's grave. Was she asking them to stay?

Union Pacific Railroad Museum

COUNCIL BLUFFS, IOWA

Council Bluffs was the eastern "Gateway to the West." Hundreds of thousands of immigrants came through Council Bluffs on their way to California. The Union Pacific Railroad Museum, located in Council Bluffs, documents those days with one of the largest collections of artifacts and documents from the nineteenth century.

The museum, which used to be a public library, has preserved some of the baggage that the immigrants carried out West. You can see the tools they carried to fix a broken wagon wheel and utensils they used for cooking.

The displays are interactive, so anyone can understand how a nineteenth-century railroad was built. Children can learn how the surveyors chose the route of the new railroad, and touch the models of nineteenth-century passenger cars, boxcars, and flatcars.

Some say that after the lights are turned off, the ghosts of the immigrants appear in the museum, never wanting to part with the belongings they had carefully chosen for their trip.

Vegor's Cemetery

STRATFORD, IOWA

This 150-year-old cemetery is nestled in a forest in what was once an Indian burial ground. When white settlers came to Stratford, they moved the Indian graves to the top of the hill. Angered that their graves had been touched, the Indians murdered a settler named Mrs. Henry Lott. She was the first settler killed in Webster County. In spite of her murder, the settlers continued to use the cemetery to bury their children and soldiers.

Visitors to Vegor's hear the voices of children laughing and the cries of the Indians. They see an apparition at the grave of Arizona, a girl who died when she was just five years old. Legend says if you look back at her grave, you will see her sitting on the headstone. But she doesn't have the sweet smile of a child. Instead, her smile is demonic. And if you stop at her grave, she will follow you around the cemetery.

Villisca House

VILLISCA, IOWA

On the night of June 9, 1912, the Moore family was in Villisca participating in the Children's Day Program at the Presbyterian Church, which Sarah Moore coordinated. Josiah (J.B.) and Sarah Moore had four children—11-year-old Herman, 9-year-old Katherine, 7-year-old Boyd, and 5-year-old Paul. After the festivities, the family returned to their home with two houseguests, Ina and Lena Stillinger, ages 8 and 12.

J.B. Moore, a prominent member of the Villisca community, had purchased the 35-year-old house in 1903. It was located in a safe, quiet community where people weren't afraid to leave their doors unlocked while they were away.

At 7:00 the next morning, a neighbor noticed that the Moores hadn't fed their chickens. She knocked on the door. No one answered, so she called Joe's brother, Ross. He unlocked the doors and discovered the bodies of the children and the parents. Each of them had been bludgeoned with an axe while they were asleep. The city marshal found the bodies of the house guests upstairs in the bedrooms.

It was the worst crime in Villisca and Iowa history. During his investigation, the marshall found the murder weapon in the room where the Stillinger children were murdered. The murderer had closed all the shades in the house. The marshal believed the murderer had hidden in a crawl space until the family had gone to sleep.

Though several townspeople were charged with the murders, none of them was ever convicted. In 1917, Reverend Lyn George Jacklins Kelly, an itinerant preacher, confessed to the axe murders. Dr. Edgar Epperly, who has made a study of the murders and has written several books on the subject, also implicated Senator Frank F. Jones in the murders.

J.B. Moore had worked for Jones at his farm implement company for several years before he opened his own farm equipment shop. Jones was upset that Moore had left him, taking his successful John Deere business with him. Was this enough motive for the murders? Moore was also rumored to be having an affair with Jones' daughter-in-law, Dona. People speculate that this also could have enraged Jones.

Allegedly, Jones hired William Mansfield to commit the crime. He was supposed to kill J.B., however, not the whole family. In 1916, a grand jury investigation began. Mansfield was arrested. But he produced payroll records that proved he was living in Illinois when the murders occurred. He was released.

Since the murders, the house has had many occupants. Bonnie and Homer Ritner rented the house during the 1930s. Bonnie, who was pregnant, kept hearing voices in the house. She told Homer, who was a day laborer and always short of cash.

It got to the point where Bonnie couldn't sleep there. Every night, she closed her eyes and saw the image of a man with an axe in his head. Her crying awakened her husband, who tried to calm her down. Their physician told Homer that if Bonnie continued to be upset she could lose her child. Homer didn't have enough money for them to move.

Then he started seeing the same images Bonnie told him about. He became frightened and tried to find the owner to ask for his money back. He ended up in the pool hall. There, the bartender showed Homer a box of bones and claimed they were J.B. Moore's. Homer ran out of the hall and rescued his wife. They packed up and left Villisca, never to return.

John and Allie Geeseman moved into the house during the '60s. They witnessed doors opening and closing on their own. They'd get up and shut the door, and it would open again. One night, while several family friends were staying with the Geesemans, the apparitions became so bad that neighbors saw the guests run out of the house in the middle of the night.

During the 1970s, the family of a trucker rented the house. While the father was traveling, his wife and children stayed in the house by themselves. Many nights, the sound of sobbing children awakened them. Often they walked into their bedroom to find their dresser drawers pulled out and clothes strewn all over the floor. One night, their father was sharpening one of his pocketknives in the kitchen. Suddenly it flew out of his hand and stabbed his palm. He had had enough. He packed up their things, and they left the house for good.

Rick and Vickie bought the house on January 1, 1974. They lived in the house for 20 years. Vickie began planting the garden with seeds from the local Girl Scout troop. The packets contained a variety of species, everything from geraniums to pansies. But when the plants began to grow, something surprising happened. One of the plants wouldn't stop growing. Called love-lies-bleeding, it grew down instead of up. The plant was a sea of red petals that reached to the ground. Suddenly, it died.

When Darwin and Martha Linn, owners of the Olson-Linn Museum in Villisca, purchased the property in 1994, they removed the vinyl siding and repainted the house white, the color it had been when the murders occurred. The pantry was restored to its original condition. Using historical documents, the Linns have also put the furniture in the same positions as on that fateful night.

In 1998, the Moore home was added to the National Register of Historic Places. It also received an award for "Preservation at Its Best" from the Iowa Historic Preservation Alliance. In 2004, Darwin Linn started construction on the barn. By 2005, after the walls were completed, the barn was finished. Visitors have signed the rafters inside. Just recently, Darwin finished the restoration of the cellar.

Darwin said that he heard children's voices during the renovation. Steve Pilchen, KGGO radio's "Round Guy," spent the night in the house after the renovation was completed. He and a few coworkers stayed in the house on Halloween. The next day, they did a broadcast from there.

Pilchen told reporters that he had experienced many different things. There was no assurance that anything bizarre would happen. He just thought it would make a fun broadcast. Just as he was going to sleep that night, he was awakened by the voices of children laughing. He thought it was just a group of kids trick-or-treating. When he walked outside, no one was there.

After a century, the Moore house continues to reverberate with the horror of what transpired there.

Woodland Cemetery

DES MOINES, IOWA

Woodland Cemetery is rich with ghost stories. For many years, it was a stop on David Ross's Natural History Tours. Some who visit it at night and stand on the outside in the same spot see two green glowing eyes. "You can't tell which tombstone it is," says David. "Some nights, the lights were there. People on our tours were freaked out when they saw the lights. We couldn't predict whether or not they'd see them. Sometimes it happened. Other times it didn't."

The cemetery holds the remains of some of the most influential people in Des Moines history. The most notable is the mausoleum of the Hubbell family, including Frederick Marion Hubbell, who created Equitable Life and Casualty. Hubbell's mausoleum is the size of a catacomb, and is the largest in the cemetery.

"Hubbell visited Rome in the 1970s and decided that he wanted a catacomb, not a crypt," says David. "Most of Woodland Cemetery's graves are catacombs rather than crypts."

There's no easy explanation for the glowing eyes. One story is that a woman's husband was unfaithful to her. Now, after her death, she sits watching him in the grave next to hers, as if to ensure that he won't do it again.

Ghostly Iowans

Brad Steiger

Brad Steiger, who was born in Fort Dodge, Iowa, is the author of more than 150 books, 17 million copies of which have been sold worldwide. He has been writing about the paranormal since 1956 and has over 2,000 articles published. His syndicated newspaper column, "The Strange World of Brad Steiger," appeared in papers all over the world in the early 1970s. His first book, *Strange Guests*, was about poltergeist phenomena. *Strangers from the Skies*, which was also published in 1966, became an instant bestseller. His wife, Sherry Hansen Steiger, is the author and co-author of more than 22 books. Brad and Sherry moved back to Iowa in the '90s, after living in New York and Arizona. They have two sons, three daughters, and eight grandchildren.

When *Strangers from the Skies* became a bestseller in 1966, Brad was teaching at Luther College in Decorah, Iowa. "It would not surprise anyone to foresee that 1967 would be my last year of teaching. The faculty may have thought I was strange before all the publishing frenzy occurred, but now everyone, including the parents who could send their children to Luther, would know that I was decidedly weird."

His book was released at the same time the Michigan UFO flap occurred. When Dr. J. Allen Hynek from Northwestern University made his famous statement attributing UFO sightings to "swamp gas," Steiger's book about UFOs was on the bestseller list for two weeks (and Hynek founded the Center of UFO Studies seven years later).

Steiger says that the attitude toward ghosts and UFOs today is much different from when he started out. "There was no cable television, with its hundreds of channels and dozens of programs on the paranormal," says

Steiger. "Since 1966, I've done dozens of radio programs, literally around the world. Usually, I average two or three radio programs a week. Each year around Halloween, I will easily do 50 to 60 hours of spooky radio. However, in over 40 years of being interviewed on radio, I've only done one interview with an Iowa station."

Steiger thinks Iowa is a great place for a paranormal researcher to live. "Iowans are nice people. The literacy rate is high, but few people read the kind of books that I write, so we are left alone. Athletes are especially revered, and their every thought, word, and deed is faithfully reported, so this leaves writers the freedom to move about completely unnoticed by the populace."

When Steiger was interviewed by an Iowa newspaper reporter in 1990, after he'd moved back to the Hawkeye State, the reporter admitted that she checked to see if the Steigers had any signs of devil worship in the house. "Since Iowa is the buckle of the Bible Belt, the residents often associate the paranormal with demonology. So one must make it clear that demons found will be exorcized, not fattened or encouraged to propagate." The same reporter couldn't believe that Steiger had written so many books, 150 in all.

"I guess it's a wonder that a native Iowan could write a single book. After all, writers live in New York and California."

Steiger believes that paranormal experiences are universal and nondenominational. He cites recent university surveys that indicate that the unchurched more than the churched have mystical experiences. Other surveys have indicated that people with more education are more open to these experiences. There may be minor cultural differences in assessing meaning and interpretation, but the mechanisms are still the same. "In my opinion, there are no *Iowa* ghosts. Or *Iowa* UFOs or *Iowa* monster sightings."

In 1972, after an article appeared about him in *Editor & Publisher*, Doubleday asked him to write a book for them. He told them that he would like to write a book about Native American spiritual beliefs, not from the anthropological approach of a college professor but from actually visiting the tribes across the United States and interviewing the medicine people. Two years later, Doubleday published his book, *Medicine Power: The American Indian's Revival of His Spiritual Heritage and Its Relevance for Modern Man*.

More recently, he has collaborated with his wife, Sherry, who is part Chippewa, on *Indian Wisdom and Its Guiding Power* (1991) and *Mystical Legends of the Shaman* (1992).

"We feel that this research into Native American spirituality has provided us with many insights into the transition between life and death," says Steiger. "There is no death, as the shaman would say, only a change of worlds."

The sharing of a mystical experience has always enriched the lives of those who hear it. Says Steiger: "At their most mystical level, ghost stories, no matter how frightening, provide testimony to the assertion that that there is something within us that survives physical death."

Steiger experienced the paranormal for the first time when he was a very young child. His near-death experience at age 11 showed him that everyone serves as a fulcrum of the universe and conduit for spiritual experiences.

Steiger says he grew up in a home with the ghosts of his great-grandparents. "It had been a stagecoach stop. I heard about the legends of Jesse James when I got older. Every night, I saw a pair of dark figures standing over my bed. I hid underneath the covers. They were stern-looking, so naturally I was afraid. It wasn't until years later that I discovered they were my great-grandparents."

His mother was a medium who received visitations every night. But his father was rational; he had to taste, touch, and smell something before he'd believe it. "He listened to our stories with interest," says Steiger. "He never criticized us." Steiger's father helped him become more skeptical about the paranormal.

The first time 20-year-old Steiger entered a room where a séance was taking place at a spiritual camp, the medium paused and told the circle that one who could become a great communicator had just entered the room.

Steiger says he's part of the old school in the way he conducts paranormal investigations. When he did investigations, he had several mediums accompany him. "These individuals were truly remarkable and would astonish police officers, caretakers, and the inhabitants of homes and institutions. And then, of course, I had my own sensitivity and the presence of benevolent beings to rely on for guidance."

"Although I have seen ghosts three times," says Steiger. "I am not a ghost whisperer. I am not a medium. And I do not help lost spirits see the light. That's not my mission. Because Sherry is a medicine woman and an ordained Protestant minister, she will sometimes do a cleansing. She is also a great believer in the power of prayer and she will pray for the departed and offer comfort to the bereaved."

Steiger has, however, devoted much of his life to the pursuit of strange phenomena, and it's not surprising that he should have high standards for paranormal investigators. Steiger says the best are "men and women who have spent years developing disciplines and discernment, men and women who are familiar with the vast literature of the field, men and women who truly know themselves, their weaknesses and their strengths." Criteria that Iowan Brad Steiger certainly fulfills.

The Nelsons and Carter House

DES MOINES, IOWA

Rick Nelson and his wife, Cindy, and their children moved into the two-story Italianate Victorian home in 1996. Years before, the house had been moved from another location in Des Moines. They had heard tales about ghosts that were believed to be haunting the place; stories about the hauntings had even been reported in the *Des Moines Register*. Still, the Nelsons turned it into a bed-and-breakfast.

"The owner warned that there was a presence there that disliked men," says Rick. "She had seen a ghost. Her husband had had a heart attack while they lived there. He watched the shower start up on its own. He also heard a man's voice."

On his first night there, Rick decided to tell the ghost a thing or two. At three a.m., he felt a presence watching him. "I thought to myself that I'd nip this thing in the bud," says Rick.

So Rick had a talk with the house. "I told the house 'I mean you no harm.'" The house responded by not bothering Rick. But the spirits did bother others members of the Nelson family and their guests.

When their house was a bed-and-breakfast, guests reported paranormal experiences. One female guest stayed in the bedroom and told Rick and his wife the next morning that the shutters were banging shut during the night.

"My wife and I looked at one another, speechless," says Rick.

"The house didn't have any shutters. It had aluminum siding, that was all. Then other guests who stayed in that room reported the same occurrence."

In 2000, when they renovated the home, they removed the siding to find wooden shutters and a closed-up window near that bedroom. The shutters couldn't possibly have moved with aluminum siding on top of them.

Other guests who came to the bed-and-breakfast also encountered a presence, but it wasn't until Allen Gardiner, a writer who was working on a book about Des Moines history, stayed in the bedroom that the ghost was identified.

"He asked if he could stay in the room for an hour," says Rick, "though he wasn't staying in that bedroom. We said OK."

When Allen came out, he told Rick that the ghost's name was Frances. She was a young girl with long brown hair, dressed in a maid's uniform. Her face was melancholy because her lover had died in the house.

"Frances inspired me to write a song," Allen told Rick, who was a musician, too. He went down to the piano and wrote out the music for what was called "Frances' Theme."

Rick's daughter, who wasn't interested in ghosts or the paranormal, told him she had seen Frances. The ghost was looking in the mirror with her melancholy face, and then disappeared. His daughter's description matched Allen's.

"I didn't know what to think then," says Rick. "Part of me thought it was solid evidence. The other part of me thought it was ridiculous."

The Carter House became part of the Natural History Tours of Des Moines, led by real estate broker David Ross. "Some of the people were so scared of ghosts they wouldn't come in to see the house," says Rick.

Rick and Cindy have researched the house's history. From its construction in 1878, it was owned by a prosperous doctor, Edwin H. Carter. After he died, his wife, Amanda, used it as a boarding house. In 1990, the house was moved from its location six blocks away and put on a new foundation. Apparently, the ghost was portable.

"We found that the house had a lot of public uses," says Rick. "The archdiocese owned the house during the '50s and '60s and held masses in it twice a day." Since Rick is Catholic and his wife a convert, they have comfort in the fact that the house had inhabitants who were priests and nuns. But none of Rick's research revealed any reference to Frances.

The house is no longer a bed-and-breakfast. None of the Nelson family has seen Frances for the past two years. In the meantime, the house appeared in the December 2004 issue of *Victorian Home* magazine, stealing the show.

The Nelsons still hope that they'll see Frances again. After all, it's her house, too.

Gaslight Ghost Tours
Randa LeJeune

DES MOINES, IOWA

Randa LeJeune, who lives in an 1873 Queen Anne Victorian at the top of the hill in the Sherman Hill Historic section of Des Moines, started her Gaslight Ghost Tours several years ago. She gathered ghost stories from the neighborhood.

"After we moved into the house, things started happening," says Randa. "I opened my tea room for business. Soon I found that a ghost was tapping me on the shoulder. We have one that touches people. The ghost even grabbed my waist from behind."

The Victorian was moved to the Sherman Hill site from the Drake University campus one mile away. Fifteen years earlier, it stood beside the Coronado apartment building. A fire there in 1977 had caused the largest loss of life in Des Moines history—five deaths. "One of those ghosts, I think, stayed with our property," says Randa. "One ghost walks down the hallway. You can hear the footsteps."

Several psychics have visited the property and identified at least four ghosts. One inhabits the guest bedroom. That ghost, according to the psychic, was the wife of a Methodist minister who owned the property. She married him at the age of 16; apparently, the experience made her dislike men in general, and she takes it out on the establishment's guests. "Men have difficulty staying in that room," says Randa. "They wake up with a headache. But married women who stay there are fine. Things get moved around in there, too."

The third ghost often appears as a shadow man dressed in early 1920s golf attire. In her research, Randa found that one of the owners was a family called Finebine that designed golf courses. "Cindy and Rick (owners of Carter House) were visiting me," says Randa. "They were doing photographs in the parlor when they heard a deep voice, a man's voice. Another time, they were putting a book away in the bookcase and saw a cup and saucer levitate."

Randa isn't disturbed by the ghosts. "It's very comforting that there are still spirits. This house is at the top of a hill in Des Moines."

When Randa moved in, during the wintertime, she got up early and saw a light fog out of her window. "I could have sworn that I saw a Native American man walking through my yard and over to the cemetery. There were no footprints in the snow," says Randa.

Five years later, her neighbor told Randa that her husband (who later had a stroke) had twice gotten up and followed a Native American through the yard to the fence of the cemetery. The Indian walked right through it.

Randa has the sites of two murders on her tour. One of them is the apartment where a woman named Ramona was murdered. Ramona moved up to Des Moines from the small town of Soap Creek in 1962. She worked a few odd jobs and lived on Woodland Avenue in a house that had been converted to an apartment building. One couple who moved in during April heard screams outside the building. A police officer was called to investigate what was going on. No one was there.

The story that's told most often in Des Moines is that Ramona was murdered by a stalker, a high school kid. One night, he climbed through the window of her apartment and stabbed her. Though the police at the time suspected who had done it, they didn't have enough evidence to convict him. The boy grew up and still lives in Des Moines, according to the story. Every year, people hear screams coming from the building.

Randa enjoys sharing her space with ghosts. Once, the ghost of her father saved her life. "I was out in the garage, where the previous owner had made a makeshift shelf. I heard my dad's voice say, 'Put on your gloves now.' I turned around and walked away, and then five minutes later the shelf fell."

It can be good to have a ghost around the house!

Tina's Stories

Imagine being surrounded by a swarm of bees in your own house. That's what Tina Carlson experienced when she was just a toddler. Tina, who was born on Halloween, has had many paranormal experiences. But she's never forgotten what happened to her in the old farmhouse in Bremer County. It was the only house at the end of a long, gravel road and was surrounded by acres of cornfields.

"I do remember telling my mother that I had seen a black mass throughout the house," says Tina, who is a co-director of Shadowlands. "Imagine a swarm of bees, and that's what it looked like. It would form out of midair and disappear as quickly."

Her mother told her that if she ignored it, it would go away. But it didn't. Tina started to cry every time she saw the swarm. Her mother picked her up, trying to soothe her. Finally, her parents decided to find a safer place for their children and moved into a smaller house in Bremer County. After they left, they heard that the farmhouse had mysteriously burned down. There were also rumors in the town about a red-haired woman someone had spotted in the second-floor window.

"I knew the rumor was false," says Tina. "The farmhouse didn't have a second floor."

Their new house had a winding staircase that led to the second floor. The living room had a front door and a small room off to the side, which her parents used as a small closet. "We only used the side door to enter this house," says Tina.

"I remember whenever my father worked nights at the plant," says Tina, "my mother would always be fearful. I never knew why. I still don't to this day." Her mother rarely allowed her to go down to the basement. Tina didn't understand why.

She has only one memory of the basement there. "I remember the shadow of a man in the basement. Not too many details. I wasn't allowed to go down there very much. It was a small room where my mother did the laundry with a wringer washer. I do remember that the man was not nice and would stand there and watch anyone in the basement. I don't think that he was a demon or anything like that, but he seemed angry or disturbed. To a four-year-old, he just seemed like a bad man."

As an older child, she learned first hand about ghosts. While her father was hospitalized, paranormal incidents increased. She and her family had been away for many days. The house was locked up. "We found cigarette butts all over the house. My mom didn't smoke. The brand was the kind you have to roll yourself. The only person who smoked in our family was my grandfather, who lived in Waterloo. He didn't have a key to the house."

Tina knew that her grandfather had visited their house while she was with her father at the hospital. Her grandfather had come there to comfort them. After his visit, her father was well again.

Tina and the Sunken Bedroom Closet

Dark shadows and heavy footsteps were part of everyday life for Tina. She'd grown accustomed to rubbing elbows with the paranormal. Each time her family moved, she had new encounters with the other side. When she was 12, her family moved into a haunted house in Bremer County. Strange, unexplainable incidents took place there year after year.

"We heard footsteps," says Tina, "and saw shadows out of the corners of our eyes. Things would disappear—jewelry, money, keys—only to turn up someplace else or not at all. After a few times, we chalked it up to our resident ghost."

She moved into the sunken bedroom, just a stairway below her parents' bedroom. One night two years before her paternal grandfather passed away, she was awakened by groaning noises coming from the bedroom closet.

"It sounded like stepping up three steps and falling down two," says Tina. "I always heard the sound in October. My mother and I joked that the ghost was trying to get up the stairs."

After her grandfather died a year later, on October 31, the sound of the heavy footsteps continued. Then on October 18, 1979, the unexpected happened. "I remember the date clearly because it was the day after my parents' wedding anniversary. My dad had just gotten my mother a dozen red roses."

Tina was in bed, listening to footsteps on the stairs for an hour. She held her breath. She could feel them coming closer. Then the sound stopped. She rolled over to face the doorway and saw a shimmering bright light about three feet wide and five or six feet tall. "It was billowing white and yellow with some other colors mixed in," says Tina.

She stood up stiffly and was reaching for the swag light when the ghostly figure walked into her bedroom. "I could see it walking towards me. I could hear it, too. I was scared to death. I could feel its total hostility towards me." When it got halfway across the room, her light came on. She couldn't see the apparition in the light. But she heard it move toward the window. The floors creaked as it moved.

"My grandfather on my mom's side had told me what to do when I get into situations like that," says Tina. "He said I should say, 'Old Tom Parker under your hat, bound in the name of God the Father, God the Son, and the Holy Spirit.' I know now, thanks to the Shadowlord Dave Juliano, that this is a binding incantation. I said this as it moved toward the window."

The figure made an unearthly moan and then disappeared. "I lay there for a few moments, trying to catch my breath, lower my heart rate, and collect my thoughts about what I had just seen. I decided to tell my parents. I got out of bed, wearing my future husband's football jersey. It was purple and came down to the middle of my thighs. Anyway, I got downstairs and turned on the light in the hallway, which cast light into my parents' room."

She ran out of the hallway and into her parents' bedroom. Tina approached her mother's side of the bed, making sure the light was on behind her because she didn't want to scare them. She quietly called her mom. Her mother turned over, still half asleep, "What is it?" She told her mother that the ghost had finally made it up the stairs. Her mother opened her eyes and sat up. The next thing Tina remembered was being thrown to the bed. She looked up and saw her father's raised fist. Her mom was screaming. Her father didn't hit her.

"We didn't see you," said her father. "We saw a four-foot-tall old woman with ratty and snarled hair white as snow down to her hips, and jagged teeth. She was wearing a long white nightgown or dress. You changed back to yourself after we threw you on the bed."

Tina's father thought that the ghost was created by his dad, an inveterate practical joker who certainly wouldn't have been beyond such a prank. For example, once, when Tina was visiting her grandfather in the hospital after he had several strokes and could barely move, he pretended to die in front of her. "I started sobbing, and he started laughing," says Tina. "He was always doing stuff like that his whole life. His number-one target was me. We were never close."

Tina remembered her grandfather that night. She walked out into the living room with her mother and father. A vase of red roses was on the table. Her father had given her mother the roses a day earlier. Her mother looked at the roses. Shocked by what she saw, she covered her mouth. The roses she had just gotten the day before were black, dead, decayed.

After that, unexpected events became the norm in Tina's house. A locked door slammed in her father's face. His keys would go mysteriously missing. Finally, Tina's father moved them to her maternal grandparents' house. As if anticipating more paranormal incidents with Tina there, her grandmother asked the deacon of their church to bless the house. When he came out of the house, he told them he didn't have the power to banish the spirits. At the end of the ceremony, he looked at Tina and said that the spirits would be drawn to her for the rest of her life.

When Tina moved out of her grandparents' house, her parents decided to put a deck on the place. They found what looked like the corner of a tombstone buried in the yard. Three years later, the house was torn down.

"The lot still hasn't been sold," says Tina. "There's been a 'for sale' sign on it for three years now. I don't think it'll be sold too soon. These events did happen to me. My life was changed forever."

• • •

When Tina's husband got out of the Marines, they needed a place to live, so they moved into a house her grandmother had been renting in Waterloo. It had no indoor plumbing; they had to pump water from a well, and a wooden outhouse stood in the back yard a hundred feet from the house.

"Shortly after moving into the house, my husband and I heard the sounds of shuffling footsteps," says Tina. "It was as if someone wore slippers that were too big and had to shuffle their feet to keep the slippers from flying off. We spent nights in bed listening to these sounds. Several times we investigated and found nothing."

Soon their neighbors in town heard about their difficulties. One neighbor, named Paul, noticed how tired they appeared. "We described the noises to him. He gave us a horrific look and left without saying a word."

Tina and her husband followed the visibly shaken Paul outside to the yard. "We spoke to him for a long time," says Tina. "It was like twisting his arm before he said that the renter had died recently. He was an old man he had become very close with."

"The one thing I remember about Jim were his slippers," said Paul. "He had a favorite pair that he wore around the house every day. These slippers were a size or two too big. When he wore them, his feet made a shuffling sound on the floor."

Tina looked at her husband. Was it Jim's ghost making those noises?

• • •

The ghostly noises weren't Tina's only strange experience in her new home town. Waterloo is a prairie town with lots of rivers that are crossed by old bridges. Tina encountered one on her way to a convenience store. She was driving a back road and passed an old sidewalk that crossed a bridge near a small creek. It had snowed the night before and it was early in the morning, so no one had used the sidewalk. She saw a woman dressed in black from head to foot on the sidewalk about to cross the bridge.

"Once you started across the bridge, there was no way to get off except by backing up," says Tina. "The bridge had a four-foot drop on either side of the sidewalk. The bridge was about 100 yards long. I was so involved in watching her that I did not see a small car coming up the cross street. She was about halfway across the bridge when the car smashed into the side of my car."

Tina got out of her car immediately to assess the damage. She saw that the right side of her car was smashed in. "The other man got out of the car and the first thing he said to me was, 'I'm so sorry, Tina. I was not watching where I was going. I was watching the woman on the bridge.'"

Tina and the man turned to look at the bridge, and she was gone.

"It would have been hard for her to ignore it, since this was a small town," says Tina. "There was no evidence that she had been there. No tracks. No footprints. She had disappeared."

Tina's ghostly experiences continue to this day. She chronicles many of her paranormal experiences on her website, www.theshadowlands.net.

Haunted Books

Bruce Carlson, a native Iowan, has written and published seven books of Iowa ghost stories, including the series *Ghosts of the Mississippi River* and *Ghosts of Des Moines County*. A chemist by education, he started off by writing a book about Iowa history.

"I found that it was hard to get it published," says Carlson. "So I decided to publish it myself. Then I broke into ghost story books. I thought that ghost stories would sell well."

Carlson created Quixote Press in 1988, naming it after the famous character in Cervantes's novel, *Don Quixote*, who believes he is called upon to redress the problems of the whole world. As he travels on his quest with his friend Sancho, he believes that the windmills are giants and a shaving bowl is a magic helmet.

To Carlson, ghosts are quixotic. You can't prove that they happened. But there is a reality to them. They are part of the local Iowa history and a treasure of our culture, handed down from generation to generation.

• • •

Carlson went directly to the source, collecting his stories from the people of Iowa. He hitchhiked throughout the state to gather them. "I began by asking people if they knew any stories," says Carlson. "I rode out into the country and stood up on a bar stool. People opened up to me."

Carlson's books focus on the type of ghost story that has a positive ending. "Sometimes the ghost warns the living person and helps him. In the type I like, there is usually a terrible act on someone's part, then the ghost commits an act of charity to someone left behind."

Recently Carlson has received requests to republish several of his titles. "We don't claim any educational value to them," he says. "But we do like the fact that librarians tell us that they're stolen from the libraries, so most librarians don't put them in general circulation." The stories in his collections don't have horrific elements, so many of his books are used in elementary schools.

Carlson used *The Twilight Zone* as his model. In the 1950s, Rod Serling often used folk tales in his television series, like Ambrose Bierce's *An Occurrence at Owl Creek Bridge,* in which the action takes place in the imagination of a Civil War prisoner one second before he's hanged. He dramatized a West Virginia folk tale called *Jess-Belle* about a country boy who becomes bewitched and marries a girl he doesn't love. Serling often wrote about ghosts returning from the grave. In *The Thirty-Fathom Grave*, a seaman is beckoned by his dead shipmates in a sunken World War II submarine. "I tend to the think that *The Twilight Zone* has elements of literature in it. It's Grade A stuff," says Carlson.

Carlson believes Iowa is a state that's rich in ghost stories because of its heritage. "It's a rural state," he says. "It's a culture in which ghost stories are very popular. Iowans are very connected to their history," says Carlson. "Folk tales, which includes ghost stories, are an important part of it." Thanks to Quixote Press, much of that ghostly history has been preserved.

Hanging in Lebanon, Iowa

Ambrose Bierce, who was a reporter for the *San Francisco News Letter and California Advertiser*, told this story, which takes place in Lebanon, Iowa, in 1853. A peddler who traveled the roads near Lebanon had stayed the night with an old man named Daniel Baker. The peddler was never seen again. Soon Baker's neighbors began accusing him of murdering his house guest.

All of this made "old man Baker" depressed. He denied their accusations even as they became more virulent. He told them the peddler, whose name was Samuel Moritz, had left early in the morning carrying his backpack and his purse filled with money. Still the neighbors wouldn't stop accusing Baker. He grew more and more isolated. At church, the women ignored him, afraid to speak to him.

After several years, the gossip died down. At that time, a Baptist minister named Reverend Cummings drove by Baker's farm at dusk. The moon was so bright, it lit up the countryside. Cummings whistled a tune as he approached the bridge. He reined in his horse when he saw the outline of a man in gray. The man had something strapped on his back and he carried a money pouch.

When the Reverend asked him if he wanted a lift, the man said nothing. Cummings got a good look at the man's face as he raised his arm and pointed to the ravine. Cummings looked down and saw nothing. When he turned his head back to look at the man, he had disappeared. His horse snorted and then led him away, suddenly terrified for some reason.

The horse was nearly at a full gallop as Cummings held on desperately to the reins. Finally, he could see that they were heading for the crest of a hill about one hundred yards away. He pulled the reins on the horse again, and the animal began to slow down. It was then that Cummings looked back and saw the figure again. Cummings believed that he had just experienced the supernatural.

When he arrived home, he told the story to his family. Two of his friends, John White and Abner Raiser, returned with him to the spot. It was there they found the body of old man Baker hanging from one of the beams of the bridge, right where the apparition had appeared.

While they were taking the body down, the men felt something strange underneath their feet—human bones, which proved to be the mortal remains of the long-lost peddler. Soon there was a double inquest with the coroner's jury, which concluded that Baker had killed himself, but Samuel Moritz was murdered by a person or persons unknown.

Alfie the Pig

The story of Alfie the pig is an old Iowa folktale. The story appears in Tom Welch's *Ghosts of Polk County*, and David Ross, the former owner of Natural History Tours, tells it to his guests as they tour the haunted sites of Des Moines.

• • •

Mr. Devlin lived in Crocker, Iowa, with his 10-year-old son, Will, who was an animal lover. He'd take in all kinds of pets, from garter snakes to guinea pigs. One year during farrowing (when the pigs give birth), their Chester White gave birth to a litter. One of the newborn pigs was a runt who was small and weak. Will named that pig Alfie and kept the name even after he learned the pig was a she.

"You should forget about that pig," said his dad.

"I'm going to take him to the Iowa State Fair," replied Will. "Alfie's going to win the blue ribbon."

His dad shrugged his shoulders. He couldn't talk his son out of keeping that pig. Soon, with Will's care, the pig grew strong, and Will made plans to take him to the Iowa State Fair. When he went to the barn one day, he saw that Alfie was gone. She had been taken with the other pigs to be butchered. He ran out of the barn, sobbing.

"You took her and killed her," he screamed at his father.

"I'll get you another pig," said his father.

"No, I want Alfie," cried Will.

• • •

Will wouldn't speak to his father for days, especially on their trip to the Iowa State Fair. The fair was crowded with people. Many had brought pigs along with them. On the main fairway, Will ran ahead of his father into the livestock barn, where thousands of farm animals were being judged in contests. He pushed his way through the crowd to see the pig in the main area. Over the pen was a sign that read, "Alfie, First Prize," and a blue ribbon.

Excited, Will grabbed his father's hand and they ran to the official desk to find out what had happened.

His father was dumbfounded. "I'm sorry, Will. Alfie was butchered. I know what I saw."

The officials at the desk knew nothing about Alfie. So Will and his father ran back into the livestock barn. Alfie was gone. But every year the kids at the 4-H pavilion watch out for Alfie. Many claim to have seen him.

The Ghost Soldier

Every community that loses its men in war has legends about their soldiers returning. The Amana Colonies are no different. The True Inspirationalists told the story of Patrick while they sat around their campfire in Ebenezer, New York. The story continued over generations after the colonists moved to Iowa. Patrick was a friend of one of the Amana families, who considered him a son.

Like many young soldiers, Patrick promised that he would return from fighting in the Civil War. After he left, stories about the war had come to the Ebenezer Colony. Many of the families had already started their trip to Iowa. But Patrick's adopted family still remained in Ebenezer, hopefully awaiting Patrick's return.

One day, eight months after Patrick had left, the father was out in the yard. He looked up from his work and saw a boy who looked like Patrick. The father barely recognized the boy, who was thin and gaunt and dressed in tattered clothes. The father ran up to him and hugged him. "Patrick," he cried. "You're home!"

The father brought him into the house to see his mother. She hugged him, and so did the children, who were overjoyed to see him. The mother fixed him a big meal made from vegetables from their garden. She gave him a large glass of milk. For dessert, she served a pie. He ate heartily, saying, "The food isn't as good as yours in the army."

While he ate, they gave him news about the Amana Colonies. They talked to him about the move to Iowa, which they were planning to do eventually.

He hadn't stayed long when he stood up from the table. "I've gotta get back to my regiment," he said.

"Stay longer," the mother said. "We haven't seen you in so long. We've missed you."

Patrick put his tattered blue hat back on. He wiped his lips with a napkin and then placed it on the table. He picked up his bag and put it over his shoulder.

"You know I love all of you," he said. A moment later he was gone.

The family talked about how much they missed Patrick. In the springtime, they left for Iowa to join the rest of the Amana colonists. That April, they received a letter from another family in Ebenezer, writing to tell them that Patrick had died in a prison camp in South Carolina. He had died around the same time as the boy—or whatever had become of him—appeared at their farmyard gate.

The Unseen Friend of the Amana Colonies

This story has been told many times by members of the Amana Colonies, though the names of the people have been lost.

During the 1950s, a family moved into a house where another Colony family had lived. Their child, Eileen, didn't like living in her new house. But after a while, she became more adjusted to living there. The house was large, with three bedrooms and a big back yard where Eileen played.

Then Eileen started telling her mother about her friend, whom she called Melanie. Eileen seemed to have no end of stories about this invisible friend. Though her mother listened intently, she was still worried that Eileen was unhappy that they had moved there.

When her mother told her father about Melanie, he said she shouldn't worry; Eileen just had a vivid imagination. After all, it wasn't unusual for children to have imaginary friends.

Then Eileen surprised her mother one day when she was ironing, telling her that she wanted to have a sunbonnet like Melanie. Her mother stopped ironing for a moment. How did Eileen know what a sunbonnet was? Maybe she had been watching too many Westerns.

Her mother forgot about it, until one day Eileen showed her a new doll Melanie had given her. It was an old doll, an antique with a porcelain face and ruffled clothes.

Her mother asked Eileen how she got it. Eileen told her that she gave Melanie one of her dolls.

Speechless, her mother couldn't imagine how Eileen could have gotten a doll like that. She might have climbed the ladder to the attic. She had only been up there once since they moved in. It was filled with dusty chests, old lawn equipment, and moldering books.

Soon afterward, Eileen came into the kitchen where her mother was stirring oatmeal on the stove. "Mommy, don't do that. You'll start a fire!" Eileen cried.

Her mother turned off the burner and ran to Eileen, trying to comfort her. Finally Eileen settled down. "Melanie told me!" Eileen said.

The next day, her mother told one of the neighbors about the strange things that were going on at the house. The neighbor told her, "You know that there was fire there that nearly destroyed the place. A little girl died in the fire."

"That's horrible," said her mother.

"I think her name was Melanie. She was only five or six."

Surprised, barely able to speak, her mother ran home and talked to her husband.

What were they going to do? They were afraid something would hurt Eileen. They both decided to move. Eileen wasn't unhappy about it. She never asked them about bringing Melanie along with them. She told them, "Melanie is staying here. She has to."

The Strange Case of the Knowles Family

David Ross, the owner of Natural History Tours, takes his guests to visit this site in Des Moines and tells them this story. This is the story of the Knowles family.

Eric Knowles' grandfather, Benjamin, owned one of the first gas stations in Des Moines. His station was located on the east side of town. Business was fairly good, so the grandfather was quite busy. A strong, heavy-set man, he did most of the work himself.

Tragically, one day Benjamin's body was discovered underneath a car he'd been repairing. He had died of a heart attack. His wife was so upset that she couldn't deal with his death. She abandoned the gas station for many years while Eric was away serving in World War II.

When Eric returned from Europe, penniless and without a job, he wanted to reopen the family business. Eric fixed up the station and hired a man named Jeff to work with him.

One day, when he was away from the station, a man with a thick beard appeared driving an old car with a stick-shift transmission. Despite its age, the car appeared to be in perfect condition. The man asked Jeff to have Eric work on the car and said that it only needed an oil change.

Eric was amazed when he saw the car in such pristine condition. He soon discovered that the car didn't need an oil change at all. He went into the back to find the papers and was shocked to discover that his grandfather's name appeared on the registration. Eric was shaking.

When Eric went home that night, he didn't tell anyone about his experience. The next day when he returned to the gas station, the car was gone.

"The guy picked it up," said Jeff.

Eric never told a soul what had happened until he met the author of *Ghosts of Polk County, Iowa*, Tom Welch. His story appeared first in that book.

Who was the bearded visitor? Was it his grandfather Benjamin? Eric believed he had seen his grandfather, though he could never prove it.

The Millville Ghost

MILLVILLE, IOWA

An elderly couple, William and Anna Meyer, had lived in their house for over 30 years before Thanksgiving night of 1959. The events they experienced there were so bizarre that they were reported in the *Des Moines Register* and a year later in *Fate* magazine.

The Meyers built this house, which rested on the banks of a small creek between two cliffs, three miles from Highway 52. William had farmed the 80 acres that surrounded the house for many years. Now 83 years old, William was immobilized with a broken hip. He sat in his chair in the corner of living room, unable to move around.

One night everything changed. While William was sitting in his chair, aching with pain, he looked up and saw powdery dust falling from the ceiling. His grandson Gene's face was covered with the stuff. So was he. It put a thin film over everything in the room.

Gene called in his father Elmer, who owned a nearby farm. When he walked in the door, his mother was sweeping up the stuff. She emptied two dustpans of it into the garbage. Elmer determined that the powder was neither ash from the stove nor dust from the ceiling.

For a while, the family joked about it. They discussed it with their neighbors. But it wasn't long before something else happened. While the family was alone in the house, they heard a big thud. After they turned on the lights, they saw that the Christmas cards had toppled off the table and a flower pot had fallen over.

But that wasn't the end of it. Anna was doused with water that came from the ceiling. She watched an egg fly across the living room and splatter on Elmer's chair. Pills showered from a bottle that was in the medicine cabinet. Mud caked the windows of the house.

Elmer thought that the cause of these strange disturbances was an earthquake of some sort. Gene didn't think his father was right. He noticed that the strange things happened when the lights were turned off. He thought it was a ghost.

After his father left, Gene turned off the lights. Then he heard several thuds. He turned on the light and found more things had fallen from the shelves and more mud on the floor.

Gene cleaned up the mess, only to find that the next day was worse. The noises were unbearable. Now the sounds were coming from the roof. It was as if there were 10 workmen up there. The noises continued for a half an hour.

A big noise erupted from the kitchen. Gene ran in there and found an old refrigerator on the floor. The bottles that were stored in it had spilled all over the floor.

The Meyers had had enough of the ghost. Gene telephoned an ambulance to take his grandfather to Guttenberg, where he could stay with relatives. William reluctantly left his house. But he told the *Des Moines Register* that if he had stayed there, he might have been killed.

Though Elmer had locked the doors of the house after everyone else had left, the doors didn't stay locked. While he was inside, a piece of wood flew past him.

Just a few days later, a group of Elmer's friends decided to spend a night in the house. Pat Livingston, who was a boat pilot, witnessed the strangest things. While they were in the kitchen, he watched the chairs move. It didn't stop there. When Pat went to bed, he soon found himself on the floor. His mattress shook. He was on the floor with the mattress on top of him. Pat left the house, shaken by what he had seen.

When the sheriff and several newspeople walked through the house in January, they saw a bottle jump up in the air right before their eyes. By that time, the haunting had gotten national attention, so the sheriff allowed some ghost hunters from Upper Iowa University to come to the house. Twenty-five students spent a night in the small farmhouse, using Geiger counters and oscilloscopes as well as ionization chambers to collect data. They stayed up all night, waiting for something to happen, checking for seismic vibrations, electricity, and radiation.

The next morning, Professor Jay Lorenz, an assistant professor of physics, told reporters that nothing unusual had occurred. The instruments had detected no paranormal causes for the strange occurrences.

The house attracted crowds. Over 2,000 people came to look and witness the hauntings. Several people, including Gene, had to be on guard to prevent the curious from invading. At times, he was afraid they'd break down the door.

That wasn't the end of the investigation. Professor Stanley Krippner came to the house on a recommendation from a professor at Northwestern University. Dr. Krippner researched the phenomena at the house and wrote a paper. He gathered information from interviews and used equipment to take readings. He concluded that the ghost came from the energy of living people. This energy caused the furniture to shift. He believed that because William was bedridden and under stress, he could have attracted this unconscious force.

When other people accused Gene of tricking his grandfather, he denied it. He said that he was not in the house when the most violent disturbances took place. To this day, the Millville ghost remains a mystery.

Glossary

apparition The appearance of a ghost or spirit, usually taking the form of a white mist.

audible voices phenomena Term for disembodied voices that can be heard by investigators in real time. (See also *electronic voice phenomena*.)

collective apparition A ghostly phenomenon seen by two or more people.

electromagnetic field (EMF) Ghosts and other entities create wave patterns of electromagnetic radiation. Paranormal investigators use an EMF detector to measure the presence of activity in a site.

electronic voice phenomena (EVPs) Ghost hunters record these voices on audio tape. Often, the researchers hear nothing as they record them. However, once the tape is played back, the voices appear.

elementals Often-malicious spirits that materialize as water, paint, or even fire. They can be confused with poltergeists, though they aren't the same thing.

ghost The disembodied spirit of a person who has died. Often the ghost resembles the way the person looked in life. Hauntings often appear to be caused by people who don't know that they are dead. Sometimes these ghosts had a violent death or committed suicide.

ghostbusters Paranormal researchers who are hired to remove ghosts from homes.

interactive ghosts Some ghosts ignore the people who inhabit the houses they haunt. Others speak to the inhabitants or tap them on the shoulder to get their attention. Also called a "reciprocal apparition."

medium Someone who communicates with disembodied spirits.

orbs White lights that are often recorded on film by ghost hunters. They are thought by some to be spirits that do not have enough energy to materialize.

Ouija board A board that has symbols, numbers, and letters printed on it, used as a tool for communicating with spirits. Users place their fingers on a sliding piece called a planchette; the planchette moves about the Ouija board, pointing out letters, supposedly spelling out messages from beyond. For more on the history of the Ouija board, check out www.williamfuld.com.

paranormal Phenomena that can't be explained by science.

poltergeist A ghost that makes playful mischief, like rapping on walls or moving items. In German, the word means "racketing ghost." A poltergeist is caused by the energy of a living person, often an adolescent who is under stress at home.

radio voice phenomenon An audible apparition that can be heard over AM/FM radio.

seance A gathering of people intent on contacting spirits of the dead, often those of dead relatives. Seances became very popular in the 19th century. They were guided by a medium who was believed to be especially adept at contacting the spirit world. The guests sat in a circle and waited for the medium to speak in the voice of the deceased.

sensitive A person with psychic abilities.

shadow man These ghosts appear to be shadows. People spot them as they are turning their head, looking out of the corner of their eye. In photos, they can be confused with actual shadows.

vortex A vortex is a strange phenomenon. It changes shape, appearing as a funnel vortex or a long, thin mist. Most often, they appear as a cold spot.

Ghostly Websites

www.diepart.com
Des Moines, Iowa, Extreme Paranormal Advanced Research Team (DIEPART)

www.iowaghosthunters.com
Iowa Paranormal Advanced Research Team
The Team researches haunted houses, cryptozoology, ghosts, spirits, and UFOs. They have investigated over 200 cases.

www.darkartfilms.com
Dark Art Films

tapsfamily.com
The Atlantic Paranormal Society (T.A.P.S.)

www.bradandsherry.com
Brad Steiger and Sherry Hansen Steiger's website. Be sure to fill out Brad's questionnaire, "The Steiger Questionnaire of Mystical, Paranormal and UFO Experience."

www.hauntedvoicesradio.com
Thomas Bates hosts this show.

www.theshadowlands.net
Tina Carlson and Dave Juliano run this popular website. The Shadowlands covers all kinds of paranormal experiences such as Bigfoot, sea

serpents, ghosts, and UFOs. They also have a long list of haunted places in Iowa.

www.translumen.net
TransLumen Technologies, LLC
Fluid stills
You can purchase a DVD of a Halloween fluid still that will make your skin crawl.

www.redicecreations.com
Red Ice Creations internet radio from Sweden. Listen to the first hour for free. The host is Henrik Palmgren from the West Coast. Henrik is an editor, musician, and graphic artist in addition to being the radio host. The show's motto is "The intelligent man will inherit the earth."

www.coasttocoastam.com
George Noory, host, covers subjects like ghosts, UFOs, and other paranormal phenomena. DIEPART members Joe Leto and Shannon Kingrey have been guests.

www.ameshauntedforest.com
The Ames, Iowa, haunted forest has a half-hour tour for people who love to be scared. The website has a coupon.

www.unexplainedresearch.com
Author Chad Lewis explores the paranormal. Find out the latest information about ghosts, UFOs, and cryptozoology.

www.hauntedworld.com
This site lists haunted areas throughout the United States. You can find Iowa haunted attractions on this site.

www.forteantimes.com
The latest paranormal news is on this site. You can watch videos and search the archives.

www.fatemag.com
Founded by Raymond A. Palmer in 1948, *Fate* magazine covers subjects like ghosts, psychic activity, past lives, Bigfoot, UFOs, and other unexplained phenomena. Readers can send in their own experiences for publication.

Bibliography

BOOKS
Bierce, Ambrose, *Present at a Hanging and Other Ghost Stories*, 1913.
Erickson, Lori, *Ghosts of the Amana Colonies*, Fort Madison, Iowa, Quixote Press, 1988.
Erickson, Lori, *Iowa o ff the Beaten Path*, Globe Pequot Press, Guilford, Connecticut, 1993.
Goss, Michael, *The Evidence for Phantom Hitch Hiker*, W.W. Norton, London, 1982.
Hein, Ruth D., and Hinsenbrock, Vicki L., *Ghostly Tales of Iowa*, Cambridge, Minnesota, Adventure Publications, Inc., 2005.
Lewis, Chad, and Fisk, Terry, *The Iowa Road Guide to Haunted Locations*, Eau Claire, Wisconsin, Unexplained Research Publishing Company, 2007.
Marshall, Alex B., *Let's Travel Pathways through Iowa*, Saint Paul, Minnesota, Clark & Miles, 1995.
Ogden, Tom, *Complete Idiot's Guide to Ghosts and Hauntings*, Alpha Books, 2004.
Taylor, Troy, *Dead Men Do Tell Tales*, Decatur, Illinois, Whitechapel Press, 2007.
Taylor, Troy, *Things That Go Bump in the Night*, Decatur, Illinois, Whitechapel Press, 2005. Welch, Tom, *Ghosts of Polk County Iowa*, Fort Madison, Iowa, Quixote Press, 1988.

GOVERNMENT DOCUMENTS
England, Otis Bryan, *A Short History of the Rock Island Prison Barracks*, Historical Office, U.S. Army Armament, Munitions, and Chemical Command, Rock Island, Illinois, 1985.

State Historical Society of Iowa, Historic Site, American Gothic House, Teacher Guide.

ARTICLES
"Cresco Theater," *Cresco Times*, Jan 26, 2007.
"Poltergeist Evicts Couple in Millville, Iowa," *Fate* magazine, May 1960.
Ballard, Larry, "Team Goes Where G-G-Ghosts May Reside," *Des Moines Register*, May 9, 2006.
Beyette, Beverly, "Fertile Imagination in Iowa," *The Los Angeles Times*, September 12, 2004.
Brown, Shane, "Iowa Ghost Hunters Visit Eastern Iowa," *Quad Cities Online*, June 29, 2006.
Brummer, Courtney, "Nonpareil Series: Hunting for Haunts," *The Daily Nonpareil*, October 26, 2007.
Brummer, Courtney, "Hunting for Haunts, Part II: Cemetery Investigations," *The Daily Nonpareil*, October 26, 2007.
Brummer, Courtney, "Hunting for Haunts, Part III: Ax House Jail," *The Daily Nonpareil*, October 26, 2007.
De la Badie, Abigail, "Shot While Trying to Escape: Confederate Ghosts in Davenport," *Third Eye Over Iowa*, Vol. 4 No. 3, March 1997.
Hanson, Chuck and Joy, "Mason Inn," interview published by About.com.
Hurlburt, Adam, "A Personal Account of Haunted Havens," *The Buzz*, October 19, 2006.
Krapft, Anne, "Spooky Fun Meets History on Night Walk (Iowa State University)," *Inside Iowa State*, October 20, 2006.
Luna, Kay, "Is Putnam Haunted? Ghost Hunters Looking for Spirits," *Quad-City Times*, October 16, 2007.
Luna, Kay, "Ghost Hunters: Putnam Museum Is Not Haunted," *Quad-City Times*, October 26, 2007.
Paluch, Tim, "Somebody You Should Know: Shannon Kingrey, Ghost Hunter," *Juice*, May 24, 2006.
Perry, Tom, "Spookologist Ranks Iowa's 5 Scariest Spots," *Des Moines Register*, October 23, 2007.
Pierquet, Greg, "The Real Ghost Busters? Not Quite," *Times-Republican* (Marshalltown, Iowa), July 20, 2006.
Randolph, Erin, "Cover: Villisca," *Des Moines City View*, February 16, 2006.
Ristau, Todd, "Haunted Iowa City: A Tour Map & Information," *Third Eye Over Iowa*, 1990.

Rosacker, Erin, "A Sesquicentennial Look Back. Historical Ghost Stories," *Inside Iowa State*, October 19, 2007.
Rosenfield, Ryan, "Historic Pottawattamie County Squirrel Cage," Historical Society of Pottawattamie County, Iowa.
Schmitt, Tom, "On the Schmitt List: Area Ghostly Tales Worthy of A Read," *The Daily Nonpareil*, October 26, 2007.
Taylor, Troy, "The Millville Poltergeist: Real or Imagination?" 2007.
Taylor, Troy, "Old Pottawattamie County Jail Council Bluff, Iowa," 1998.
Taylor, Troy, "Prairie Ghosts," 2001.
Tirpitz, Eugene, "The Black Angel's Thumb," *Third Eye Over Iowa*, Vol. 4 No. 2, December 1997.
Tudor, Sean, "Road Ghosts" *Fortean Times*, No. 73, February/March 1994.
Warner, Jarod C., "The Black Angel: Iowa City's Most Mysterious Monument," *Third Eye Over Iowa*, Vol. 3 No. 10, October 1996.
Warner, Jarod C., "Haunting of Currier Hall," *Third Eye Over Iowa*, Vol. 3 No. 10, October 1996.

WEBSITES
www.americanghosts.com
www.bbs.thekeyhold.com
www.binellofamerica.com
hotels.about.com
    The Mason House Inn
www.darkartfilms.com
www.darkhavenentertainment.com
www.desmoinesriver.org/kshelley.htm
    Kate Shelley
www.diepart.com
www.dmcityview.com
www.ghostlytalk.com
www.ghosthunterstore.com
www.groups.msn.com/IowaCenterforParanormalResearch2/hauntedplaces
www.hauntedhouse.com
www.hauntedplaces.com/Iowa
www.haunted-places.com
www.horrorfind.com
www.iastate.edu

www.iowacenterforparanormalresearch.com
www.iowaghosthunters.com
www.iowabeautiful.com
   Mathias Ham House
www.legendsofamerica.com
www.irishmidlandancestry.com
   Kate Shelley
www.kcrg.com
www.kwwc.org
www.midiowa.com
   Central Iowa Ghosthunters
www.nonpareilonline.com
www.outofthestatic.com
   IPART radio
www.prairieghosts.com
www.qctimes.com
www.radioiowa.org
www.realhaunts.com
www.thegrandoperahouse.com
www.thejordanhouse.com
www.thirdeyeoveriowa.com
www.unexplainable.net "Haunted Cemeteries throughout Iowa"
www.whotv.com
www.yawp.com

ORGANIZATIONS
Amana Heritage Society
   www.amanaheritage.org
Des Moines, Iowa, Extreme Paranormal Advanced Research Team
Des Moines, Iowa, Historical Society
Dubuque County Historical Society
Historical Society of Pottawattamie County
   www.thehistoricalsociety.org
International Ghost Hunters Society
Iowa Center for Paranormal Research
Iowa Genealogical Society
Iowa Ghost Hunters
Iowa Historical Society
Iowa Paranormal Advanced Research Team
Iowa Sesquicentennial Society

Iowa Tourism Office Museum of Amana History
State Historical Society of Iowa
The Atlantic Paranormal Society (T.A. P. S.)
The Putnam Museum
The Shadowlands

DOCUMENTARIES
"The Amana Colonies," Iowa Public Television
"Greenwood Cemetery," YouTube
"Villisca Murders," YouTube

www.ingramcontent.com/pod-product-compliance
Lightning Source LLC
Chambersburg PA
CBHW070102080526
44586CB00013B/1154